Survival
Driving

Survival Driving

Staying Alive on the World's Most Dangerous Roads

Robert H. Deatherage Jr.

Paladin Press • Boulder, Colorado

Survival Driving:
Staying Alive on the World's Most Dangerous Roads
by Robert H. Deatherage Jr.

Copyright © 2006 by Robert H. Deatherage Jr.
ISBN 10: 1-58160-554-4
ISBN 13: 978-1-58160-554-9
Printed in the United States of America

Published by Paladin Press, a division of
Paladin Enterprises, Inc.
Gunbarrel Tech Center
7077 Winchester Circle
Boulder, Colorado 80301 USA
+1.303.443.7250

Direct inquiries and/or orders to the above address.

Graphics help provided by Devanie Flaska of Freedom Graphics, 1923 Woodbine Road,
St Joseph, MO 64506 (freedom @stjoewireless.net).

Thanks to Dave Bowman and Frank Willoughby for reviewing my work.

Visit our Web site at www.paladin-press.com

Contents

Introduction

Vehicle security is one of the most important aspects of life when living in high-threat areas. As Americans, we have become used to traveling by automobile, and we take this habit with us when we travel overseas.

We also have a false sense of security in our vehicles, thinking we are invulnerable as we go about our daily business. After all, we have learned how safe our vehicles are and how well they protected us while we lived and worked in the Untied States, where laws governing how we drive, the quick response time of emergency services, and the design of the vehicle might afford us some protection in accidents.

However, this is not true when you become the target of a threat that is determined to kill you, kidnap you, or somehow make an example of you. After all, President John F. Kennedy, Austrian Archduke Franz Ferdinand, German industrialist Hans-Martin Schleyer, Lt. Col. Charles Ray, Lt. Cdr. Albert Schaufelberger, and Col. Nick Rowe were all killed while in their vehicles, and President Ronald Reagan was just a few paces from his vehicle when he was shot and badly wounded by John Hinckley Jr.

The methods discussed in this book concentrate on ways to prevent attacks before they happen. But if an attack does happen, this book will teach you how to escape by first using your vehicle as a weapon and then escaping in it. I hope that it will give you a new insight into things you can do to protect yourself and your family while traveling, either overseas or in the States.

A note about gender is in order here. Although victims, as well as terrorists and criminals, can be male or female, for the purpose of brevity, we have used the pronouns *he* and *him* throughout this book when the gender of the individual is unstated. You should consider these terms gender-neutral.

CHAPTER 1

Who Is a Target?

People become victims of terrorist or criminal attacks in several different ways. Some threats are easy to avoid and some are not, depending on such factors as the type of business you are in, the reason you are in an area, and the amount of publicity surrounding you.

People can be either general or specific targets. First I will discuss general targets.

GENERAL TARGETS

The three most common ways people become general targets of terrorist or criminal acts are being in the wrong place at the wrong time, getting targeted through association with someone who is a target, and becoming a target of opportunity.

Wrong Place, Wrong Time

This is just like it sounds—being in a place at the same time an attack takes place. This type of attack does not target you specifically, but rather is aimed at a particular location. Terrorists often target places where Americans gather on a regular basis— such as bars, hotels, stores, and eating establishments (e.g., fast food places that are common in the United States)—because they are reminded of home. If you are travel-ing to an area where your company has had a long-term presence, avoid spots that are known as hangouts for foreigners, since they will likely be targets already. To avoid becoming an unwitting victim of a criminal act, avoid banks, jewelry stores, or high-class shopping areas, which are probably already under some type of surveillance by criminals looking for easy targets, regardless of nationality.

Victim by Association

Sometimes you associate with people who are already targets because of their occupation. This could be someone in a high-profile position, such as chief of security, or it could be any employee of an industry that terrorists have historically targeted.

You might have to work with or meet with government officials, city leaders, business leaders, and law enforcement personnel in the course of your daily activities or duties. If they are targeted, then you (or the person you are protecting), when in close proximity or association to the intended target, could become involved, regardless of the victim's status or perceived security. Be aware of whom you are meeting and where, and try to determine if these types of people have been targeted or threatened in the past.

If you are going to conduct meetings with locals, find out how they are perceived in the community and if there have already been attacks or threats against them or their interests. This will help in adjusting your security profile when meeting or doing business with them.

Target of Opportunity

Being a target of opportunity is very similar to being in the wrong place at the wrong time, except the attackers are looking for someone who doesn't fit in, e.g., a nonlocal. It doesn't really matter who, just any foreigner with a weak security posture who can be attacked in some way—and there you are.

A good example is the targeting of vehicles driven by foreigners in Iraq by roadside improvised explosive devices (IEDs). Terrorists wait for a certain type of vehicle to pass and then explode the device. The attackers don't really care who they get, but they know from experience that only foreigners or Americans drive certain types of SUVs or other vehicles, so, boom, you are their next target of opportunity.

SPECIFIC TARGETS

Most people are general targets, but what if you are targeted for a specific reason? People on potential target lists are put there for many reasons, nationality being a common one. Terrorist organizations have preferred target countries, because they are trying to influence those countries' foreign policy or politics, whether it is America, Israel, Britain, or Spain. Organizations that target people by their country of origin are not concerned with your occupation and will target you while you are vacationing, passing through, working, or doing volunteer or relief work in a country.

Both terrorists and criminals identify targets based on their perception of certain people's importance to the business interest, government, or other organizations in that country. When I talk about the threat perception, you have to understand that targets are selected based on the perception of what people outside your sphere of security see, not on what *you* know. A person looking at you, your organization, or your client knows

A common weapon against targets of opportunity is the IED. Avoid becoming a target by blending in with the locals.

Your vehicle might not look exactly like local vehicles, but the less it looks like a military vehicle the better. Bigger is not always better.

only what he can see. If you look or act like an important person, then to him you are. It is important to stay as low profile as possible and not let someone outside your sphere of security think you are important enough to be a potential target.

You or your client might be a very important person (VIP), but while traveling you need to discourage any activity that will make you stand out to people in general. This includes receiving special treatment at the airport upon arrival into a country, such as being greeted by local authorities or business executives or getting escorted through customs control points or baggage areas. Other signs that might telegraph to a criminal or terrorist that you or your client is a worthy target are carrying luggage or equipment that stands out, having a limousine or other type of conspicuous vehicle waiting for you, and having an escort. Such things will make you stand out as different, and because you are different you are important. Remember to keep that low profile.

Many foreign hotels offer their guests the use of cars and drivers while they are staying there. These cars usually stand out compared to what the local population drives. Criminals or terrorists see the car and reason that people who have access to these special cars from the hotel must be important. Or your business or the embassy might send a

car and driver to take you around. Once again, this will also make you stand out and possibly identify what your interests in that area are or for whom you work, which could also make you a potential target.

If you are planning on staying or living in an area for a considerable time, look at leasing a vehicle instead of buying one. But be aware that many countries give foreigners license plates that are different than those of citizens of that country. For example, Germany puts the American flag on the plates of Americans' vehicles. You want to avoid having your vehicle, which normally blends in to the local environment, stand out because of its license plates.

Decals and stickers on your vehicle can also place you on a target list. Some businesses, organizations, exclusive housing areas, clubs, and schools require them for access and parking. Not only do these types of decals tell curious parties where you live, shop, or go to school, they may also identify you as an important or wealthy person. Kidnapping is a major source of income for criminals and terrorists in some countries, and targeting people or corporations that have the money to pay is always inviting. If your job site, club, living area, school, or business requires this type of identification for access, ask if you can place the permit on an index card and keep it in your glove box when not in use. This will lessen your profile on the street during movement and make your vehicle more difficult to pick out when it is parked in public places.

Individuals who have chauffeurs or drivers are considered important, so do your own driving whenever possible. If you don't know the area initially, or the security threat is such that you must have a detail to protect you, then a driver should be considered a part of your security profile. But if the driver is not essential for security purposes, use one only until you become familiar with the area and the routes, and then decline his services and obtain a different car. If your position requires that you have a permanent chauffeur, make sure he is trained in security and defensive driving. You should decide which routes to use, what speed to drive, and the departure times. You should also change the type of vehicle often to confuse any surveillance. Remember, whenever you have someone else behind the wheel, you are placing your life in his hands.

Only someone who believes he is important or considers himself at risk will have a bodyguard or security detail. The more important the person is—or thinks he is—the larger the security detail will be. Keep the number of guards during transport to the minimum number necessary to meet the threats for that area. As a general rule, a security detail for transporting you should blend in with the rest of the population so that people cannot tell how many there are in the detail, the types of weapons they have, and where they are in relation to the person they are protecting. If you deny this information to the criminals or terrorists, they cannot plan for it. Be unpredictable; raise that security profile; be that hard target.

On the other hand, if you know you are a target, then having a visible security element will raise your security profile and make you a harder target for the threat. This is good, since attackers prefer softer targets. If your position, job, or status is such that you know you will be a target no matter what you do, you must never allow yourself or your security detail to get complacent. You need to make it as difficult as possible for the threat.

By firing first at an actual or a perceived threat, security details have sometimes forced would-be kidnappers into becoming assassins. A good security detail will move its principal out of the area as soon as a perceived threat is presented, firing only when necessary to clear the way and neutralize those blocking the escape. In some cases, bodyguards have killed their own principals during firefights because of poor training and experience. Make sure that the individuals guarding you have trained for every conceivable scenario. Then be proactive in planning for your security.

Another way to identify someone who may be important is to see where his vehicle is parked. Even if you have done everything correctly to ensure that you don't stand out in any way, if you park in a reserved spot or have access to a special parking garage or area when you get to the plant or office, it makes all your other precautions worthless. Remember that the threat will have some type of surveillance at the work site, and a reserved parking spot that identifies you by job title or position makes you an instant target. This goes not only for work but also for clubs, restaurants, theaters, and hotels. Maintain a low profile by avoiding special parking areas.

Having a personal assistant who answers the cell phone for you, carries your briefcase, or sees to your needs will mark you as a potential target. After all, only important people have personal assistants.

What you carry with you during your day, whether for leisure or work, can also identify you as someone who might be a potential target. We have all seen people who can't seem to turn off their cell phones, personal digital assistants (PDAs), or laptop computers. Contrary to popular belief, not everyone has these devices or uses them everywhere, especially in certain foreign countries. The type of briefcase you carry can also make you stand out. One with real leather, your initials, or brass fittings will make you look like someone with money. If you travel with items like these, place them in your trunk or out of view. Better yet, choose an inexpensive briefcase and carry all your other items in it. If you must have that expensive briefcase or high-tech device, buy an innocuous-looking backpack/day-pack and carry it in there. Remember, anything that makes you look important or wealthy could make you a target.

Anything that identifies you by name or schedule (e.g., television, newspaper, or magazine coverage with your picture or projected arrival dates or itineraries, such as speaking engagements and dinners) will make you a possible target. And who knows who will see the article or news clip and how the information conveyed will be used? The fact that you are in the news already means you are an important person and a potential target.

Airplane loading manifests tell the air-lines which people sit in what seats, such as first class and business. Who knows what happens to this information in countries where privacy laws are lax?

Immigration, customs, and country arrival forms also have the potential of pro-viding more information to interested parties than you would like: the hotel where you are staying, your permanent residence, contact phone numbers, and the reason you are visit-ing. Although these forms may be required, you should be as vague as possible since (as with other forms you fill out) you don't know who is going to see them and what they will do with the information.

How you dress and act overseas can help identify you as a foreigner and a potential target. Many people don't think anything of wearing expensive clothes or jewelry, carry-ing expensive bags, flashing large bills of American currency, or having multiple credit cards in their wallets when they travel. Depending on where you are, such conspicu-ous behavior could make you a victim, especially of a criminal act. It would be fool-ish to get yourself injured or killed because you wore a Rolex or an expensive pair of jeans into the wrong area.

You should always be thinking of how peo-ple are going to perceive you. If you are aware and alert, people will see your heightened awareness and view you as a hard target. Because terrorists or criminals have certain characteristics in common, we can know what criteria they are looking for in a target or vic-tim. One of the most important factors is a target who presents little or no risk to the per-petrators, as well as a very high probability of success. This is especially true for terrorists. When terrorists fail in a high-profile act, their organization or cause receives bad publicity, which affects their support and recruitment efforts. For criminals, failure may mean jail time, which is something they wish to avoid.

So your goal is to have others perceive you as a hard target, which equals a lot of risk involved with very little chance of suc-cess. This book will show you how to harden yourself as a target during your most vulner-able time, which is when you are in a vehicle moving between locations, a situation where you have no control whatsoever over the environments you are moving through.

UNDERSTANDING YOUR SECURITY PROFILE

Personal Security

❑ Do you and family members leave for work, school, etc., at the same time each day?

❑ Do you and your family leave work/school to return home at the same time each day?

❑ Do you have regularly scheduled meetings that involve travel (e.g., having to attend meetings at different office sites throughout the week)?

❑ Do members of your family have regularly scheduled activities (e.g., children's sporting events, wife's dinners, school plays)?

❑ Do you need to travel outside a secure area for lunch?

❑ Are there any primary areas you stop at on a regular basis on the way to or from work (e.g., coffee shops, newspaper stands)?

❑ Do you maintain an exercise schedule or other recreational activity (e.g., jogging, tennis, golf) on a regular basis?

❑ Do you frequent shops, stores, restaurants, theaters, car washes, etc., on a regular basis?

❑ Do you attend meetings, social get-togethers, or school events on a regular basis?

❑ Does anyone in your family attend night school or have hobbies that require him to be outside a secure area on a regular basis?

❑ Do you or family members attend religious services on a regular basis?

❑ Do you attend professional sporting events on a regular basis?

❑ Do you have one day set aside for household chores (e.g., shopping for groceries, laundry drop-off, pet grooming)?

❑ Do other family members have regularly scheduled activities that require your presence?

❑ Are there any other activities you or your family engages in that make you time or place predictable (e.g., walking the dog, going outside to get the morning paper or milk deliveries every morning)?

Travel Security

❑ Do you and others in your family have a standard mode of transportation? If so, what is it?

❑ Do you or your family members ever vary routes on a random basis?

❑ If you do vary your routes, do you do it in a predictable way (e.g., when it rains, taking a certain route because it is easier to drive; when you are running late, taking a certain route because it is quicker)?

❑ Do you have an assigned vehicle from work, or can you take any vehicle you want from a motor pool?

❑ Do the assigned vehicles you use stand out in any way (e.g., stickers, colors, styles, official markings, special license plates)?

❑ Is it possible to rotate vehicles with others on a random basis?

❑ Do the vehicle's style and type blend in with what is driven in the areas you will be traveling through?

❑ Do you have a regularly assigned driver?

❑ Do you have the same driver every day, or can he be changed out without your knowledge or consent?

❑ What type of verification process do you have to ensure that a new or substitute driver works for your organization?

❑ Do your driver and other security personnel speak and understand your language?

❑ Do you speak and understand theirs?

❑ Do your driver, secretary, and other employees know your travel plans, routes, and routine for the day in advance? If so, how far in advance?

❑ Have you established some type of code so your driver can let you know when he is under duress, and it is not safe for you to enter a vehicle or leave a safe area?

❑ Is your driver armed and qualified with the weapon he carries?

❑ Does the driver inspect the vehicle thoroughly before picking you up?

❑ Has your driver ever received any type of driver's or security training? If so, what type?

❑ Have you ever received any evasive driving or security training?

❑ Have you ever received any surveillance detection training?

❑ Has your driver received training in vehicle bomb search techniques and IED recognition?

❑ Does your driver stay with the vehicle at all times while it is parked on public streets, in public parking, or other nonsecure areas?

❑ Do you have access to secure parking for your vehicle at night and while you are at your primary locations (e.g., workplace, health club)?

❑ Does your vehicle receive regular maintenance by a qualified and trustworthy individual?

❑ Is your vehicle equipped with a two-way radio?

❑ Are there places along your traveling routes where your cell phone or radio does not work?

❑ Do you have body armor, and do you understand how it can be defeated?

❑ Do you wear your personal protective equipment (e.g., body armor, helmet)?

❑ Is your vehicle armored? Do you and your driver understand its capabilities, how it can be defeated, and the necessity of keeping the vehicle moving to maximize the vehicle's protective capabilities?

Routes

❑ Do you have at least three different routes so you can vary your route to and from work and all other primary areas?

❑ Do you vary your routes?

❑ Do you know how many choke points exist on each route and their boundaries?

❑ Have you identified your critical navigation areas?

- ❑ Have you prioritized the choke points and critical navigation areas in terms of how valuable they will be to an attacker?
- ❑ Is it possible for surveillance to be conducted in these areas for the time required to develop an attack plan?
- ❑ Can you be controlled long enough in these areas for the attack to be effective?
- ❑ Have you identified the most likely covers or ruses your enemies would use to operate in these areas and how long they can maintain these ruses or covers?
- ❑ Have you identified whether the attack will be a standoff or close-in attack, based on the layout of each area?
- ❑ Do these areas offer any other tactical advantages to the threat?
- ❑ Do they offer any tactical advantages to you?
- ❑ Are there any escape routes in these areas?
- ❑ What types of attacks has the threat carried out in the past?
- ❑ Do you know the most likely position for surveillance in the choke points and critical navigation areas?
- ❑ Do you have a plan to detect this surveillance in these areas?
- ❑ Have you identified the best attack sites along each route?
- ❑ Is one of these attack sites near a choke point? And is that near your residence or work?
- ❑ Do you or your security always check with the correct officials or companies about the validity of utility crews in your attack sites, choke points, critical navigation areas, and the areas right before you enter each?
- ❑ At the potential attack site, choke point, and critical navigation area, will varying your times make a difference in the environment, lessening your chances of being a target?
- ❑ Do you know how much of a time difference it would take, and can you make the adjustment?
- ❑ Do the choke points or critical navigation areas meet the requirements for a good attack site, using past threat attacks as a reference?
- ❑ Can your high-threat areas be covered by countersurveillance or surveillance detection?
- ❑ Can the lead vehicle in a convoy or motorcade travel through these areas at least 30 seconds ahead of you?

CHAPTER 2

The Weakest Link

The most dangerous time for most people in their daily lives is when they are in their vehicles moving between locations. They already have lots of things on their minds; they are worried about being on time, traffic, daily schedule, etc. Being this distracted means that they usually don't have the time or energy to pay attention to what is going on around them.

This commute is especially dangerous when it is in a high-risk or high-threat area, since vehicle travel is the *weakest link* in your security chain. You are leaving protected areas that a threat cannot penetrate and venturing into public areas, where you have no control and where you are playing on the same field as your pursuers. Therefore, it is vital that you learn what is going on in the area you are traveling through before you leave your safe area.

When the International Association of Chiefs of Police reviewed more than 4,000 terrorist attacks, it found that the terrorists were successful 91 percent of the time. Even when the target was considered hardened or protected, terrorists succeeded 87 percent of the time because of the victim's complacency, routine, attitude that "it has never happened here before and it won't happen to me," and shortcuts with security procedures.

Threats are quick to take advantage of any security weaknesses when you are traveling. It doesn't matter what the travel is for, whether for business, family, or pleasure, as pointed out by Carlos Marighella in *Minimanual of the Urban Guerrilla* (first published in 1969 and still available from Paladin Press).

A number of security problems are always present with vehicle travel, including the fact that a vehicle can be easily recognized by year, make, model, and color. Look at the protective details now in use in the Middle East. Most use big SUVs, which make it much easier to see over a greater distance but which also stand out from the local vehicles. Someone with training can usually accurately assess the modifications made to vehicles, including armor and radios, and they can plan for any security measures that they can identify. That is why it is important to look at the environment you are working in. If everyone is driving around with highly visible security and armored vehicles, then these things are no longer deterrents. They are now expected, and the attackers will find ways to neutralize those tactics because they have to target someone to get their message across or achieve their goal.

In these circumstances, it might be better to keep a low profile compared to the other people working in the environment and find ways to keep your potential adversaries guessing. It is better to avoid being the target of an attack than to survive three or four attempts.

Terrorists or criminals also have resources available that allow them to use surveillance to build a target folder on you. These resources also make it possible to practice repeated dry runs of potential attacks at different locations with a very low risk of detection. This enables them to anticipate any problem areas and plan for them, thus enhancing their chances for success when they do actually attack. While traveling in your vehicle, you will have limited resources upon which to rely, and people often become focused on fixed security manpower, armored vehicles, and speed. This works in favor of the threat, who is better geared for mobility and can develop a plan to overcome any obstacles your security plan presents and thus to accomplish the job.

So in this book we will look at ways to increase your security to the highest level possible. Some proactive measures you will learn to do include thorough route surveys, route analysis, surveillance detection program, attack recognition, how to counter surprise, immediate action drills, and vehicle evasive maneuvers (e.g., attack the attacker, J-turns, reverse out, PIT, ram).

CHAPTER 3

Route Analysis

The first and most important link in your security chain will always be awareness of the threats you face so you can take measures to protect yourself or your client. This means you must become familiar with the general threats in the area and the specific threats against you—how they operate, and their history, tactics, procedures, and past actions. Will they use IEDs anywhere, or do they like to limit the collateral damage of civilians? Do they use vehicle-borne IEDs (VBIEDs)? Do they prefer drive-by or vehicle-overrun attacks? Finding the answers to these and other questions will give you a better idea of what you are up against and how to start planning your security.

The most important thing you can do to ensure your safety while traveling by vehicle is a route analysis. A route analysis examines all the routes you use to travel to and from your primary areas. A primary area is anywhere you spend time on a regular basis (e.g., home, work, satellite offices, airports, restaurants, bars, clubs, gyms, movie theaters, grocery stores, day-care facilities). A good route analysis will minimize the threat of attack during movement, because the time and place of an attack can be predicted with a very high degree of confidence. An attack will most likely occur on a part of your route

that cannot be varied and near a choke point or other vulnerable area. Most attacks against vehicles occur near the residence, most often in the morning during the initial trip to whatever primary area the victim is moving to. This is when people are the most predictable in their daily lives, and it is when you should be most careful. It is harder for attackers to predict actions in the afternoon and evening hours, since these times are controlled by other events that happen throughout your day. You should be careful, however, not to let yourself fall into a predictable pattern of arriving home, going out for dinner, or picking kids up from day care at the same time.

For all primary areas, you must have a minimum of three routes to and from them. Since people cannot be totally alert 100 percent of the time, routines and boredom can result in a bad security posture; trying to stay fully alert 100 percent of the time will just wear you and your detail down. With a properly done route analysis, you will know when and where the possibilities of being attacked are greatest, allowing you to increase your awareness in those areas at the necessary times and locations. By having a preplanned response for those areas, you will lower the chances of being surprised, which, in turn, will help you execute the necessary maneuvers to get out of the danger zone.

MAP RECONNAISSANCE

First, you must conduct a map reconnaissance of the area you will be traveling in. The focus will be on the primary areas where you intend to travel, the roads you will be using, and the three separate routes you will be taking to those primary areas. This means you will need to acquire as many different types of maps as possible and satellite photography of those areas identified. Fortunately, satellite photos are easily obtained from commercial imagery Web sites for a reasonable price. Study all the maps and images you have, but don't try to memorize the entire city. Learn its patterns, major thoroughfares, cross streets, and high-volume traffic areas and times. Find those places that look like they will be congested at peak times, have three roads intersecting at one light, have traffic lights on every block, or are located on a road with many on and off ramps.

Now look at your primary areas and start looking for routes. Don't worry about the length of the route; you are looking for major features, parks, airports, office buildings, and public parking areas. While analyzing these routes, you need to locate potential safe havens (places you can go that have their own security or law enforcement, or where you can expect to get assistance or at least repel any pursuers, who will want to avoid confrontation with outside elements). Examples include police stations, hospitals, government buildings, banks, fire stations, churches, jewelry stores, and embassies.

RESTRICTIVE TRAVEL AREAS

Once you have identified safe areas, you need to look at those areas that can be potentially hazardous or restrictive. This will include any site that might impede your movement or provide cover to the threat. Spots to avoid include public gathering places (e.g., parks, universities, schools), impoverished or high-crime areas, any road that passes by a political party headquarters, or any other locale you think meets the criteria, based on your initial research into the area.

Choke points or critical navigational areas are spots that can control or inhibit your movement and that you must pass through at some point. Your route should contain as few choke points as possible, and the choke points themselves should be short. Two choke points for most people involve

The trash and debris along this roadway are possible hiding places for IEDs. The mosque in the background could either be a possible safe haven along this route or a place to avoid because of religious or ethnic tensions. Your intelligence of the area should tell you which.

their residence and their work site. Remember, you will have no control over the areas surrounding these sites; once you leave you only have control over your own actions. Examples of choke points are toll booths, traffic circles, one-way streets, narrow bridges, cul-de-sacs, entrance and exit ramps, drawbridges, school zones during school hours, narrow streets, twisting roads, hills, and blind spots in the road.

PREPLANNED CRISIS RESPONSE

Now you need to write down each route, describing it in detail and noting the starting point, the direction of travel, any safe areas, suspected choke points, and the total distance in miles. You also need to come up with a preplanned crisis response for each choke point: what you are going to do, which direction you want to go and which you do not want to be forced to go, who to call for assistance that will be closest to that area.

When planning your response, you need to be especially observant around choke points to make sure that there is no way around them. If there is a way around them, you can take it off the list of choke points. You also need to confirm that your safe areas are still in operation, their business hours, how to access them when you need to, and the type of protection or help they will provide. Then you will need to think about how your preplanned crisis response will work, taking into consideration all the information you now have.

Now comes the fun part: you need to drive the routes you have identified, using your notes to see if the maps are accurate and if your preplanned crisis response is feasible. You need to maintain a log (a tape recorder or video camera can help with this) as you or your security team members drive each route at each time of the day you think you will likely drive it. In this log you should note distance, road surface composition, effects of climate changes on those roads (e.g., does the street department have a snow or ice policy that designates the road as one-

way while blocking off others?), whether traffic lights are synchronized, whether there are actual traffic police directing traffic at intersections, temporary construction on roads or buildings along the route, potential loitering areas (e.g., bus stops or outdoor restaurants), types of vehicles being driven in the area, and traffic patterns.

You will then go home and write down your notes, listen to the tapes, or watch the videos. You must do this with all routes to each of your primary areas.

Even with all this preparation, people still routinely keep habits useful to a potential attacker. When the attacker selects an attack site, he will choose a point where the victim is predictable in terms of place and time. This is true even if your security varies your route daily for every trip, because on every route you take there are two portions that cannot be changed: the beginning and the ending points. Most frequently these will be home as the starting point and work as the ending point, but they can vary. The trip could be from work to the gym at 5:00 P.M. on Monday, Wednesday, and Friday. There will probably be choke points along these routes that cannot be avoided, and your attackers will discover these through their surveillance.

TRAVEL SURFACES

The terrain you have to travel on will affect how you can move about your area of operation and is a critical part of your route analysis. Understanding how the terrain will affect your vehicle is vitally important for planning your daily movements and your preplanned crisis response.

Hard-surfaced roads are always the best to move on because they provide excellent traction and maneuverability. But be sure to check how weather affects these roads. For example, do they have adequate drainage? During high winds, is an excessive amount of sand or dirt blown onto the roads? If so, it could affect how your vehicle responds to commands. Sand and soft dirt can act like talcum powder or water on a hard surface and cause your tires to lose contact with the road surface and slide.

The best type of traction for a dirt road is one where the soil is moist but not soaked. Dry dirt roads have good traction, but they will cause lots of dust and can impair visibility if you are following other vehicles. When they get very wet, dirt roads without gravel just turn into mud pits. So be wary until you have driven a dirt road in that condition. You do not want to get stuck when you are under attack.

Sand acts pretty much the same way as dirt or soil. When it's very dry, a sand road can be powdery and dusty, so it will put lots of dust into the air also. But very dry sand is something you can sink through, depending on its depth and the base beneath it. Wet sand offers the best traction, but very wet sand is like mud.

Drive on each of these surfaces during different types of weather so you can evaluate each on its usability. Remember that some of the above road characteristics could be beneficial if you are being followed or pursued. A dry dirt road would be an obstacle for someone following you because the cloud of dirt produced would impair his vision. Traveling on a gravel road will throw up rocks that might shatter the windshield of a pursuing vehicle. The other side of the coin is that if you are pursing or following someone, these surfaces would have the same type of effect on you and your vehicle.

WHERE ARE THE ATTACK SITES?

After you have a route description and have driven each route and know the location of all the choke points and safe havens, and the types of road surfaces, next comes another important step in preparing your route analysis: an analysis of each possible attack site, which are usually very close to your choke points. Doing this will give you a clear understanding of where and when the possible attack sites will start and end, which will allow you to maintain peak alertness at those critical times and places and to control the element of surprise. During this phase you need to think like the bad guy, based on information you have about your enemies and their past attack profiles and tactics, and put yourself in their shoes.

Determine the advantages and disadvantages that each attack site offers the threat. Do your schedule and selected routes cause you to arrive at the attack site routinely? In other words, are you time and place predictable at some point during your daily routine? Is the attack site well defined? Does it permit an attacker to limit your actions and responses or otherwise gain control of you? Is there cover and concealment for the attackers themselves (remember, they need a way to blend in and a reason for being at that particular place at the right time, so is there a plausible reason for an individual or group to linger or loiter at the site, such as assembling in the park, standing around a lunch truck, or standing at a bus stop by a stoplight)? Is there favorable terrain for an attacker, places that hide the threat from you? Finally, can the attackers quickly and easily escape the area after an incident? Is there unobstructed access to major thoroughfares? Are there multiple streets available from that site? Is there an alternate means of transportation available? Are there areas they can just blend in to and walk away?

Write down your thoughts and observations on each possible attack site. The attack site that gives your enemy the greatest chance of success and best meets all his criteria will be your most dangerous area. (See Chapter 13 for specific attack scenarios and Chapter 16 for case studies of actual attacks.)

TYPES OF ATTACKS AT VARIOUS SITES

Now that you have identified where the attack sites will most likely be, it is necessary to consider the type of attack that will probably be used against you, based on what is available at the site and the tactics your adversaries have used in the past. Bad guys always use tactics that have been successful for them because doing so makes them feel comfortable. Each site will be a little different, and once again you will have to think like the bad guys. Can they do a standoff attack with a rifle or rocket? Take out your vehicle with an IED? Use a drive-by attack with a car or motorcycle? Does the area provide enough concealment for stopping the vehicle and kidnapping you, or stopping the vehicle and doing an assault against it?

Once you have looked at everything and studied your observations, you will need to readjust your preplanned crisis response to fit those scenarios. You need to constantly think about your actions and visualize what you will do as you approach those danger areas. When you do this, it shortens your reaction time to surprise so you don't panic and can activate your escape plan more quickly.

So what exactly is the threat looking for when searching for an attack site? For the purposes of this book, we will consider four general types of attack sites: urban static, urban moving, rural static, and rural moving. We will also look at the specific requirements for using standoff weapons (e.g., RPGs, light and heavy machine guns, sniper weapons). Your route analysis should take the requirements for each of these into consideration.

Urban Static Attack Sites

- The location should support surveillance by the attackers over an extended period.
- It will probably be an area where you are time and place predictable.
- A narrow cross street where the target vehicle does not have room to maneuver is ideal.
- A traffic control point (such as a stop sign or signal) will cause the target vehicle to slow down or stop.
- The threat will have the ability to control (isolate) the attack site.
- The farther from police stations or other security, the longer the reaction time will be to an incident.
- Multiple side roads and cross streets mean the attackers have multiple escape routes.

- The area will allow attackers to blend in to the environment before the attack.
- The area lends itself to the use of a ruse (e.g., a mother pushing a baby carriage across the street, a car accident) to slow or stop your vehicle.
- This area allows attackers to stage vehicles for the attack and then get away quickly.
- The target's view will be obstructed, such as from trees or hedges.
- There is little or no traffic.
- The attackers have the ability to communicate or pass visual signals to one other.

Urban Moving Attack Sites

- The street is wide enough so that an attacking vehicle can pass on the driver's side of the target vehicle.
- The attack area has several open roads or side streets for the attackers' escape route.
- There is little or no traffic to interfere in the attack and the escape.
- Vehicles need the ability to communicate to coordinate the attack and escape.
- The area is located away from emergency services and law enforcement.

Rural Static Attack Sites

- The terrain must be favorable to the attackers.
- Cover is available to the attackers.
- The attackers have a good field of view and field of fire available.
- The attackers can use a blind curve, sharp turn, bridge, or other routine feature to set up a roadblock to force the target vehicle to slow down.
- A roadblock must be placed so that it cannot be observed until it is too late for the target vehicle to turn around.
- A roadblock must be able to obstruct the road enough that the target vehicle cannot pass or go around.
- There is little or no police or other security presence.
- The area lends itself to many ruses, such as broken-down farm equipment or vehicles, or animals on the road.

- The attackers have the ability to communicate with radio equipment or visual signals.

Rural Moving Attack Sites

- Any type of vehicle—including motorcycles, all-terrain vehicles, and pickup trucks—can be used.
- A two-vehicle attack is likely, with one passing to get in front of the target vehicle and control his speed and the second pulling up on the driver's side of the target vehicle to initiate the attack.
- The attackers need a clear, straight road with little or no chance for the target vehicle to drive off the road or turn. Therefore, ditches or fences along the road are a must to help control the target.
- There should be little or no traffic to interfere with the passing maneuver and the attackers' escape.

Attack Sites for Standoff Weapons

- Positions from which the attackers can positively identify the target and stay hidden until the firing starts are essential for standoff weapons to be used.
- The attackers need clear fields of fire so they can track and follow through with the attack.

- Standoff weapons also require an elevated position, a stable platform to shoot from, and in the case of the RPG-type weapons a back-blast area.

This means that in the urban environment you need to keep an eye on the rooftops, baseball fields, or any other areas that provide the necessary requirements. In the rural environment, you need to check for elevated areas on either side of the road, especially if they provide cover and concealment. Examples include fields that have been cleared recently, small hilltops along the road, and radio towers where people can observe your approach and warn the attacking element. So whenever approaching these areas, raise your awareness level and be prepared for anything.

• • •

Remember, as the target *you* dictate the time of attack, place of attack, and type of attack! It is your routine, your route, and your security profile that the threat plans for. The easier you make it for your attackers, the more likely that you will turn into a statistic. The following checklist summarizes what you need to prepare your route analyses to make yourself a hard target.

ROUTE ANALYSIS

❑ *Have you identified three routes to all your primary locations?* The best routes to choose are ones with easy movement, few or no stops, nonwinding roads, few danger areas and choke points, and safe areas or havens along them.

❑ *Have you identified safe havens along all routes and primary areas?* A safe haven is a place that ideally is open 24 hours a day or, if not, is open when you will be driving by. It should have people around who can provide assistance or intimidate a pursuer, some type of communication means (e.g., telephones, radios), and possible medical assistance. Suggested safe havens are police and fire departments, embassies, banks, hospitals, truck stops, and jewelry stores—basically any location that has its own security. Research identified safe havens in advance so you know what type of help is available at each location and what is required to use it or gain access to it in an emergency. Safe havens should be marked on a map or map overlay.

❑ *Have you identified choke points and danger areas where vehicular movement is restricted and you are forced to slow down, or your movement and speed are dictated by some other means outside your control?* Examples of choke points include bridges, tunnels, S-curves, one-way streets, construction zones, traffic lights with long wait times, stop signs, traffic circles, blind curves, narrow or winding streets, culverts, and congested traffic areas. Areas that you must always pass through to get to one of your primary areas are choke points or areas of predictability. You must travel these because you have no other option. Examples include a single road into a cul-de-sac, a single road that must be taken to get to a highway, dead-end streets, and traffic circles. Choke points and danger zones should be marked on the maps of everyone who will be using those routes. In a danger zone, movement is not only restricted, but additionally you may have to stop due to circumstances beyond your control, and concealment is available to potential attackers. If there are obstacles present (such as new construction, delivery vehicles blocking the road, or an accident), this becomes a possible ambush point. In a rural environment, it could be animals on the road or broken-down vehicles. You need to look at the whole situation.

❑ *Have you identified travel times and distances to all primary areas and safe havens for each route?* Annotate this information on a map for all routes.

❑ *Have you identified hospitals throughout the routes and time and distances to them?* Hospitals should be identified not only as safe havens but also for emergency treatment. Some hospitals may be acute-care centers and may not be able to treat all conditions; however, they can treat minor injuries and stabilize life-threatening injuries. Other hospitals are full-trauma, level-one hospitals that can treat all conditions. You should consider the type and severity of the injury and medical attention needed when deciding whether to seek medical treatment or move to a more secure safe haven. Locations of the hospitals and times and distances to them should be marked on a map or map overlay.

❏ *Have you identified checkpoints along the route?* A checkpoint should be something in the terrain that is visible day or night in any weather. Good checkpoints include skyscrapers, cellular towers, railroad crossings, large bridges, and stadiums. Observing checkpoints along the way gives you and your driver the ability to monitor and inform security personnel what the closest checkpoint is in case of trouble.

❏ *Have you identified observation points for conducting fixed-site countersurveillance along your routes?* An observation point is a location, such as a terrain feature, where covert observation may be conducted over portions of the route that have an increased chance of risk. This location may be a building, a hill, or even a sidewalk restaurant or hot dog stand, as long as your security will have an unobstructed view along that portion of your route. These are very important for your security plan.

CHAPTER 4

How to Overcome Induced Panic and "Fight or Flight"

Few things in your life will be as dynamic and overwhelming as the violence inflicted by terrorists or criminals. Earlier I told you the high success rate of terrorist attacks against their targets. Now I am going to tell you why the rate is so high.

Surprise is one reason, and it is the goal of every ambush or raid. When your enemy achieves total surprise, you are caught unaware. This causes you to hesitate, disbelieve, and think about what is taking place, trying to come up with a solution. This can cause *induced panic,* another factor in favor of the terrorist. Avoiding panic is why you do such a thorough route analysis. That way you have an improved idea of where an attack can take place and can prepare yourself mentally by raising your awareness levels.

At the time of an attack your body is reacting to being startled. Several involuntary chemical reactions take place to increase your chance of survival. Have you ever been badly scared by someone you didn't see, or have you ever been in a near-miss accident? Think about how you felt—your heart raced; you became aware of everything around you; you instinctively turned from the perceived threat. You did all of this unconsciously. That is the fight-or-flight syndrome.

Nature has given each of us a variety of tools to enhance our survivability when we are confronted with danger. The fight-or-flight response is our body's primitive, automatic response to prepare the body to fight or flee from a perceived threat to our survival. We all need to understand this response better so we can add it to the tools to use in our defense.

Research and study have shown that when we experience excessive stress (induced panic)—whether from internal worry or external circumstance—our bodies automatically respond with a series of events designed to protect us from perceived threats and bodily harm. First researched by the Harvard physiologist Walter Cannon in the 1920s, this response, which is hard-wired into us, takes place in an area of our brain called the hypothalamus. When stimulated, the hypothalamus initiates a sequence of nerve cell firings and chemical releases (including adrenaline) into our bloodstream. This dump of chemicals causes our body to undergo a series of very dramatic changes. The respiratory rate increases. Blood is shunted from our digestive tract and directed into our muscles and limbs, which require extra energy and fuel for running or fighting. Our pupils dilate, and our sight sharpens.

Our awareness intensifies. Our impulses quicken. Our perception of pain diminishes. Our immune system mobilizes with increased activation. We become prepared both physically and psychologically for fight or flight.

The fight-or-flight system bypasses our rational mind, where our more well-thought-out beliefs exist, and moves us into "attack" mode. As such, we tend to see everyone and everything as a possible enemy. This is meant to buy us time while our mind is attempting to cope with the perceived threat that startled or surprised us. The stress produced when danger is present can cause your mind to overload. This fight-or-flight response kicks in by not requiring our mind to deal with the threat it is facing; it is interceding to allow an enhanced response to the threat.

Threatening situations do not always cause the fight-or-flight response to kick in or maintain, however. If you perceive that you do not have a chance for fight or flight, then another defense mechanism can kick in. This mechanism decreases heart and breathing rates and takes actions to conserve energy. This response can result in your fainting or freezing up from fear, which makes you a much easier target.

So now that you have an understanding of what your body is trying to do, you need to know how to control these reactions to your benefit. The way to overcome induced panic is through training, rehearsals, knowledge, and maintenance of your awareness levels so you can take appropriate actions when necessary. Since surprise itself is a frightening stimulus, in an already high-threat situation it can get you killed. By finding ways to limit the enemies' ability to surprise you or induce panic, you take away one of the most dangerous elements in their planning. That is one of the reasons you do a route analysis: to predict possible attack sites and methods so you can raise and lower your awareness levels as required. Hopefully, this means you won't be surprised and can react with quick, rational thinking to escape the threat.

So what if the attack still happens even after all your precautions? Remember, the odds may be against you, but with good route and attack site analysis and a well-practiced crisis response, your chances of surviving go way up. If you don't remember your preplanned response, just remember the most important thing you can do in a vehicular attack: *move.* Do not become a stationary target; get out of the killing area as fast as you can. Studies of past attacks have shown that terrorists plan for a specific "kill zone," and if the targets aren't in the zone—either because they turn away before they reach it or they move out of it quickly—the attackers will flee.

If you are attacked, there may be a moment when you question either fighting or fleeing. If the incident has deteriorated so much that any type of resistance will bring death, then you need to consider not resisting. The important thing to remember is that your choice must be a conscious one, not an involuntary reaction to the situation or no action at all. Don't become a news headline because you do nothing.

CHAPTER 5

Awareness

What is awareness? Awareness is being able to "read" situations around you and make an assessment of what is taking place or about to take place. Awareness is one of the keys in your ability to detect attacks and lower the element of surprise.

Awareness is *not* about being fearful or paranoid. It is a relaxed state of alertness that needs to be used in your everyday life. You need not be in a heightened state of awareness at all times; your awareness levels should be adjusted to meet the perceived threats of your environment. This will allow you to react more quickly. In this chapter, we are going to go over the different levels of awareness so you'll have a better understanding of how aware you need to be throughout your daily routines, especially during movement from one area to another.

GUNSITE COLOR CODE

The Gunsite Color Code was developed and taught by Jeff Cooper at the Gunsite Academy in Arizona in the mid-1970s. It relates to the degree of peril you are willing to do something about and which allows you to move from one level of mind-set to another to properly handle a given situation. The

code consists of four mental states, which Cooper expressed in colors: Condition White, Condition Yellow, Condition Orange, and Condition Red.

I have attempted to adapt this code to movement by vehicle. During such movement, your state of alertness will fluctuate, and it is important for your security to be conscious of the degree of alertness during potential or actual threatening situations. Your level of awareness will directly influence your ability to detect threats, respond to them faster, and effectively gain control of perceived threats in your environment. It also helps you to maintain self-control and keep a focused mind during a threatening encounter.

Condition White

This is a state of environmental unawareness and is the condition most people are in naturally. While in this condition, you have no idea what's going on around you because you are daydreaming, tired, distracted, or unaware of the possibility of trouble and thus feel no cause for alarm. Take a look at people walking down a busy city street or driving around you—you'll see that about 80 percent of them are so wrapped up in their own worlds that they don't realize what's going on around them.

You should maintain a Condition White level of awareness only when you are at home or in another safe environment where you can relax. Never be at Condition White when you are outside your safe areas and moving to another primary area.

Condition Yellow

People in Condition Yellow are aware of their surroundings. In this state, you are relaxed but alert, cautious but not overly tense. You maintain an easy but continuous 360-degree sphere of observation of the people, vehicles, places, things, and actions around as you scan the immediate area and make eye contact with people close by, including drivers of other vehicles. You are not expecting a hostile act, but you are aware that aggression is possible. Because you are constantly evaluating your environment, you are in tune with it and responsive to any signals that might suggest a potential threat.

Condition Yellow is the minimum level of awareness to be maintained during those times when you are traveling to and from your primary locations. Condition Yellow is not being paranoid, just operating from a level of increased alertness, which people around you—especially your enemies, who might have you under surveillance—can perceive. Your discernible alertness will increase your security profile in their eyes and could convince them not to attack you.

Condition Orange

The change from Condition Yellow to Condition Orange comes when you recognize a potentially dangerous situation (e.g., a specific threat, vehicle, or person) and move into a state of alarm. You have decided trouble is imminent and are evaluating your situation to determine the best course of action available to you. Your options will depend on your training, experience, and any precrisis planning you have done. You need to stay in control and not allow yourself to act without thinking. Use your plan; move to one of your safe havens.

Condition Red

In this condition, a potential danger has now become an immediate threat to you. Reaction to the threat is necessary for your survival. Now you are in fight-or-flight mode; you need to neutralize the threat or move. Your body's systems kick in, and your adrenaline levels and heart rate are at their peak. Stay focused while in this condition; you need to keep your presence of mind. You should not be making knee-jerk reactions; you should be basing your responses on the threat, your training, your knowledge of the area, and your preplanning.

AVOIDING PANIC

The last aspect of awareness that we are going to talk about isn't really one we want to train for. This is the last thing you want to happen—being so startled that you become totally unresponsive to a threat. Without any type of training or preparation for crisis situations, you run the risk of moving straight from Condition White to induced panic. This must be avoided at all cost! Panic leads to misdirected frenzy, which can produce paralysis. You become a nonmoving target, so surprised that you can't even think to duck. By changing your awareness and perceptions as you move into different levels of danger, you should be able to avoid the induced panic that is one of the biggest weapons your attackers can use against you.

No person can maintain Condition Orange or Red for any lengthy period; it's too intense and too mentally exhausting. You preplan and do route analysis so you know when you are moving into those potentially dangerous areas. You heighten your awareness so you can stay in Condition Yellow when a high level of awareness is not needed, because it can be sustained indefinitely without excessive strain. You must remember, however, that just being in Condition Yellow is no guarantee that you will spot the danger in time or assess it accurately. But it does allow you to read your environment better and lets you move in a controlled, conscious manner through the response levels as needed.

By knowing what areas are potentially dangerous for you, training yourself and doing your preplanned crisis response, and visualizing different attack scenarios and the responses for them, you greatly diminish the threat's ability to surprise or panic you. Therefore, your reaction to the threat will be greatly enhanced.

SECURITY AWARENESS

- ❑ Know the threat.
- ❑ Be aware of your location at all times.
- ❑ Practice surveillance detection all the time, at every location.
- ❑ Be at your highest level of alertness when entering or leaving your vehicle.
- ❑ When outside your vehicle, stand facing it, which offers the greatest view of the exterior.
- ❑ Be suspicious of anything that causes you to stop your vehicle.
- ❑ Don't stop to help anyone; use a phone and call for help.
- ❑ Plan ahead while moving; play the what-if game.
- ❑ Do not allow yourself to have a routine or become time or place predictable.
- ❑ Know the routines, vehicles, and people in your neighborhood and around your work sites.
- ❑ Use major thoroughfares, roads, and streets when possible.
- ❑ If stopped, move as quickly as you can around the obstruction.
- ❑ Always be on the lookout for any situations where your vehicle may become blocked, and take preemptive action.
- ❑ Take note of and report any unusual activity as soon as possible.
- ❑ Know all your choke points, danger areas, and zones of predictability, and be extra alert when approaching these areas.
- ❑ Never assume that someone else is aware of and taking care of an issue when it comes to your personal security.
- ❑ Always assume that the worst will happen and have a plan for it.
- ❑ Rehearse all your emergency action plans, at home, en route, and at the office; the more you practice, the quicker you will be able to respond.
- ❑ *Do not become complacent!*

CHAPTER 6

Attack Recognition

You now have a good route analysis and know the choke points and possible attack sites. You know the threat's methods of operations and tactics, and you have an understanding of how surprise figures into the attack and how to counter that surprise using the color-coded levels of awareness.

How will you actually know when you are being attacked—when the bullets start flying? If you are going to survive a well-planned assault, early recognition is essential. The unwary person arriving at the attack site has very little chance of surviving or escaping. But because you have identified what you think are potential attack sites and have raised your awareness levels to coincide with the danger possible at those areas along your route, you will not be caught unaware.

At the attack site, the advantage goes to the attackers because they know the time and place of the attack, the methods they will use, and how they will get away. You will have to counter each of these, and if you are unwary, you will more than likely be unable to. But the threat also has disadvantages, and these can make the attack sequence recognizable and give you a heads-up of any impending attack.

While driving, you need to be observing all that is going on around you, not reading or playing with the radio. You need to be watching as far out as you can see, which might enable you to see the attackers setting up or preparing for you. But don't forget to observe to the rear of the vehicle, and make sure to keep other vehicles out of your blind spot. You are looking for any suspicious activity in and around the choke points or possible attack sites that you identified in your route analysis. As you approach these choke points and danger areas, move into Condition Yellow and mentally go over your options, your preplanned response, and where the safe havens are located for that area. If you observe suspicious activity, stay as far away as possible or turn around. Be especially observant of nonverbal communications taking place around you: from vehicle to vehicle; from a vehicle to a person or persons standing on different street corners; from cars passing and flashing lights somewhere in front of you and then turning off suddenly or pulling over, but not letting anyone out; or from people paying too much attention to your vehicles as they pass.

As you leave your primary areas and move onto your route of travel, start looking for correlating activities from the environment and the people. Correlating activities are actions by the attackers that are cued by your movements. I discuss correlating activities in detail in the next chapter on surveillance detection, but I want to mention them here briefly.

So what correlating activities should you be looking for? Watch for movement that keys off you or your client, or vehicles that are waiting for you to approach to pull out. The same goes for people; look for people who are pacing your vehicles and seem intent on getting in front of or beside you. Notice whether they pass up opportunities to cross the street before you arrive.

The threat must maintain communication so that personnel know when and how you are approaching the target zone. You can use this to your advantage by being on the lookout for people who, as they watch you, are talking on the phone or into the radio and looking at their watches.

One of the attackers' main disadvantages is that they have to switch from the disguise that allows them to blend into the environment to their attack persona. That transition is what you should be looking for as you approach any identified danger areas. For example, the person is sitting, but as you approach he stands and starts moving toward your vehicles. Or the person is leaning against the wall holding a bag, and as you approach he starts moving toward you, pulling something from the bag as he gets closer.

Indicative behaviors to look for in people who are waiting to transition into an attack mode include the following:

- Shifting weight or acting nervous
- Glancing furtively at and then away from the possible target
- Dressing inappropriately for the location or weather (e.g., a costly suit in the inner city or a coat on a hot day)
- Wearing clothing that is too loose
- Carrying bags, luggage, backpacks, or other types of containers that do not fit in (e.g., a golf bag when there are no courses in the city)

- Keeping hands in pockets at all times, regardless of weather
- Patting, touching, or looking at coat or bag, as if checking to make sure everything is there
- Having a pale face that is obviously from recently shaving off a beard
- Being unresponsive to other people in the environment (e.g., ignoring direct salutations, looking around people who get in the line of sight to the target)
- A group of people noticeably focusing on the target's approach and not acting like a normal group of people (e.g., conversing, laughing)
- Sitting or standing rigidly, which could indicate the person has something strapped around his midsection or hidden under his coat (such as a bomb or a rifle) that prevents normal movement
- Clenching hands, as if holding something he is afraid of

I discussed the types of attacks in detail in Chapter 3, but to help you spot a switch from innocent bystander to potential attacker, I will reiterate a few points here. You should watch for any actions that could signal the following types of attack:

- *Close range with personnel.* This is the typical ambush using people on foot rather than in vehicles. Watch for people transitioning into an action mode as you approach, or other correlating activities.
- *Close range with an IED.* Being intimately familiar with your operational environment will help you spot this type of attack as you approach danger areas or choke points. Are all the normal vendors out? Are children normally present at this location and time, and are they there? Are the shops open and outside tables filled with the usual number of people? Is the farmer grazing his livestock next to the road as usual? If there is any change—anyone missing, businesses closed, roadside vendors absent, or other usual things

that are missing—it might be a good idea to stop and go back or go around.

- *Standoff attack.* This attack uses some type of direct-fire weapon to target you specifically when you enter the kill zone. It could be a sniper with a rifle or some other type of shoulder-fired weapon. But to use such a weapon, the threat needs room to use it, and a clear field of fire, so keep an eye out for locations that offer these conditions. Be aware that this is a very difficult type of attack to detect beforehand.

CHAPTER 7

Surveillance Detection

A study of the phases of criminal attacks reveals that the majority occur *only* after a certain period of surveillance by the threat. Therefore, a formal surveillance-detection program should be an integral part of your overall security program. It is especially important if you consider yourself at high risk or you work in a high-risk environment. Since surveillance is the visible part of the threat, this is your greatest opportunity to confirm or deny whether you have become a target and may even help identify the threat before an incident can take place.

Early detection of surveillance is important if you are to know when you have become a target so that you can take the appropriate protective measures. Once you understand the objectives, phases, and surveillance techniques commonly employed by terrorist organizations, you will be better equipped to detect surveillance and possibly prevent yourself from becoming a victim.

Setting up a surveillance-detection program for you, your family, or your clients is very simple and can be done in two different ways. The best way is to get training for you (or your client), the family, staff, and security personnel in surveillance detection, and let them observe as they go about their daily routines and duties. The second way, if you have the money and resources, is to contract with a company to provide this type of service on a full-time basis or to hire your own separate, beefed-up security staff to provide surveillance detection and countersurveillance services. But even with this second option, you need to train everyone in the household in surveillance detection. As I said, the first option is better, especially if you have been working or living in the area for a long time, because you already have some of the local information required to detect things out of the ordinary.

Before undertaking either option, you must understand what surveillance is. A good definition is the continuous or periodic act of observing, usually by surreptitious means, a person, a place, or an object for the purpose of obtaining information otherwise unavailable or impractical to obtain.

SURVEILLANCE PHASES

As with everything else your attackers do, there are multiple phases to their surveillance operations. The two most notable phases are target selection and assessment, and operational/attack.

Selection and Assessment Phase

During the selection and assessment phase, surveillance may or may not be as professional as that conducted by a government intelligence service. However, even the most well-trained individuals make mistakes, giving the wary target a chance to detect surveillance personnel. The purpose of this phase is to allow the threat to gather information to discern patterns in the target's daily activities or routines. This is also when the threat will prioritize the list of potential targets, deciding who offers the greatest chance of success with the lowest degree of risk. The terrorists will then use this information to determine the security awareness level and precautions being taken by the target and a possible time and place for the actual attack.

This is the earliest and weakest phase of surveillance, primarily because of two factors: terrorists will normally use newer, less-experienced members since the surveillance team may have to pass a police or other identification check, and they need more people so they can look at several different potential targets. The surveillance generally continues for a substantial period, giving the trained observer several opportunities to detect the agents.

Operational or Attack Phase

In the second phase, the operational or attack phase, the terrorists have chosen their target based on which candidate offers the best chance for a successful attack. The surveillance will now become much more-professional as better-trained and more experienced members of the organization take over. It is no longer necessary to maintain constant surveillance on the target, as his daily routines and other patterns have already been established.

What type of information is the threat looking for when selecting a target and planning an attack? Terrorists have two goals they want to achieve through surveillance: (1) establishing the target's day-to-day routine to determine predictability, and (2)

evaluating his personal security posture. Most groups prepare target lists and then conduct surveillance to eliminate those potential targets who are unpredictable or who have good security practices. Brig. Gen. James L. Dozier, kidnapped by the Red Brigades in Italy, was that terrorist group's third choice as a target for kidnapping. Dozier was predictable and exercised poor personal security, while the two higher targets had good security and weren't predictable. (See Chapter 16 for more information about Dozier's kidnapping.)

Terrorists will attempt to gather the following information about potential targets.

- *Target's residence and workplace.* Statistics show that most attacks occur near the home or the workplace, because it is very difficult for the target to remain unpredictable near these locations. It is important, therefore, that the terrorists gather as much information as possible on these locations so that they can become intimately familiar with the surrounding area. Their specific operational plan will be quite different if the target resides or works in an urban area rather than in a rural environment. An unlimited number of variables come into play when the terrorists look at the terrain from the perspective of cover and concealment, avenues of ingress and egress, possible choke points, and other considerations likely to affect their tactical planning.
- *Target's mode of transportation.* The planning scheme will differ greatly if the target normally travels by bicycle rather than car. On the other hand, the target may rely primarily on public transportation systems and taxicabs. If the target is prominent, he may use motorcades with a lead vehicle, a chase vehicle, or both. In these instances, the specific type of public transportation system or the automobile the target uses will certainly be of interest to the terrorists for identification and planning purposes. Also they will need to know whether the vehicles

are armored and whether the target or his security agents carry weapons.

- *The routes the target travels to and from work and other primary areas frequented on a regular basis.* Examples include church, theaters, restaurants, bars, or health clubs. Such information is very helpful to the threat. For example, operational planning will be quite different if the target travels over rural, isolated, or neglected routes rather than major thoroughfares in urban areas. One-way streets, traffic lights, blind curves, narrow roads, etc., will all influence the terrorists' operational planning to one degree or another.

- *The target's behavior.* This is the most important type of information, because a person's everyday actions will have the strongest impact on whether he is a hard or soft target. Without a doubt, the more predictable the potential target is, the easier it will be for the terrorists to do their operational planning. A careful study of the numerous successful terrorist operations in the past two decades shows that the target's easy predictability made these operations relatively simple.

- *The target's general security awareness.* If he is totally unaware of the general threat in the area or denies that it exists, the terrorists' job will be much simpler. The ruses, tactics, and techniques employed by the threat to gather information will not have to be as elaborate or clandestine in nature as they will if the target is security conscious.

- *The general character or tone of the target's neighborhood, work environment, favorite places, and travel.* This will determine the type of surveillance personnel employed by the terrorists and what their manner and dress will be. Naturally, a person who frequents loud bars and inexpensive restaurants in more common neighborhoods will require a different type of surveillance than one who attends the theater and frequents exclusive clubs and expensive dining establishments in well-to-do surroundings.

- *The protection systems employed at the target's residence and workplace and on his person.* Examples of fixed site protection systems include closed-circuit television with motion and heat sensors, dogs, roving patrols, and silent alarms. Examples of personal protection devices include weapons, bodyguards, and vehicular security systems.

- *The types of security forces in the area that are likely to react to an attack on the target and their reaction times.* Do the police agencies have units trained in counterterrorist operations, or are they merely traffic-cop types with little or no special training? Are government armed forces likely to take part in operations against the attackers? This information will play a significant role in when, where, and how the terrorists decide to attack the target.

Surveillance is more than just following people. For terrorists, it means finding out as much as possible about critical areas so they can determine whether a target is soft or hard, which is then used to gather the information needed to plan their attack.

TYPES OF SURVEILLANCE

There are four general types of surveillance: fixed site, moving, technical, and a combination of the different types. I will discuss a little about each to help you understand better what is taking place and how the threat uses them when working against you.

Fixed Site

Fixed site (also called stationary or static) surveillance targets a fixed location, such as your house, work site, choke points, or other primary areas. To evaluate your vulnerability to fixed-site surveillance, you need to put yourself into the mind-set of the terrorists: "Where would I have to be located to observe all avenues to my house, my office, and my routes to and from those identified choke points?" When you do your research on terrorist or criminal groups in the area, you should determine whether they like to attack a target when he is en route or entering or leaving a fixed location. This will help you identify where you need to concentrate your observation for locating possible surveillance. Remember, most attacks take place near the target's residence, because that part of the route is not as easily varied. Also most people are more vulnerable in the morning when departing for work, because morning departure times are more predictable than evening arrival times.

Fixed-site surveillance is probably the most common and preferred method for terrorist organizations. It does not require as much skill as mobile or en route surveillance and, therefore, is not as easily compromised.

The surveillance team will seek a position that permits them to observe the residence or office clearly without being observed or suspected. This may be done from an apartment in the area, a van, or a parked vehicle, or on foot. Even though the surveillance team will attempt to watch unobserved, they must come up with a plausible reason for being in the area in case they are detected. Pretexts can include being a new vendor, renter, shop owner, or employee.

To detect fixed-site surveillance, you first need to know the problems that surveillance agents will have to deal with. *The first rule of surveillance is that those doing the observing must maintain visual contact of the subject.* Surveillance does no good if the agents can't see you. They are unable to control your environment, so basically they will be reacting to everything around them, including you. All people who conduct surveillance fear being detected; ironically, this fear often causes them to do things that make them stand out so that they are easier to detect. They are often placed in unfamiliar, uncomfortable situations over which they have little or no control, so all kinds of things could come up. There is also the problem of inactivity. After all, watching a building during the day, waiting for the victim to do something, isn't a whole lot of fun, and the

surveillance personnel have to deal with such problems as boredom, hunger, fatigue, bathroom visits, TV, radio, girls walking by, etc.

Now that you know some of the things that your adversaries have to deal with to keep you inside their areas of observation, you know what to look for and be aware of. But you should also know that the hardest type of surveillance to detect is fixed site. It's important that you use your knowledge of the area—which includes the geographical, social, criminal, and cultural characteristics—to help you identify individuals who do not belong there. Observe those places from which surveillants can observe you! This will help you eliminate tangential areas and concentrate resources where you need them.

Before leaving a fixed site and going mobile, you need to observe the surrounding area for about 15 minutes. Observe the environment during your departure and make sure someone at the departure site is also observing as you leave, and for at least 15 minutes after you depart. Among the things you are looking for are any correlating activities, such as cars that leave as you do, people who exit buildings and get into cars going in the same direction as you are, people taking notes or photographing or videotaping where it seems inappropriate; and vendors who close shop and leave just as or just after you do. This is one of the big mistakes that agents make when conducting any type of surveillance: allowing their immediate correlating movements to tip off the target.

Another thing you need to keep in mind when attempting to detect surveillance from a fixed location is that surveillants will do everything they can to blend in and remain undetected. Therefore, you or trusted employees must become intimately familiar with what is "normal" in your area so you can recognize anything that is out of the ordinary. In other words, you must know the personalities and the profiles of your surrounding environment. One way to do this is to maintain a neighborhood pattern analysis for each of your primary areas. This is nothing more than a sketch map of your neighborhood, detailing such things as types of vehicles used by your neighbors; at what times they normally leave, return, or in general conduct their daily business; and where they park.

It is also necessary to be knowledgeable about vehicle license plates indigenous to your particular area. As with the different license plates for each state in the United States, most countries have either a numerical or an alphabetical system to differentiate between cities, provinces, etc. Learn to recognize those that are out of area.

Also know which service vehicles and personnel are normally in the neighborhood and at what times they are usually present; locations of manhole covers and telephone and power mains; the regular presence, times, and locations of vendors; and any other information that could alert you or your security team to any suspicious changes in one of your primary areas.

Some of the common places used for fixed surveillance are hotel/motel rooms, apartments, houses, offices, businesses, and mobile vendors. Remember that whatever location the surveillance team chooses, it must provide an adequate view of both the area to be surveilled and the target—that means they have to be in a location where they can observe you and your daily activities. Although seldom easy to acquire, a fixed location provides the people doing the surveillance with the best defense against detection. But acquisition of a fixed location invariably leaves a paper trail back to the terrorist or criminal organization.

When canvassing hotels for any suspicious activities, surveillance-detection or security personnel should check out guests who demand a room that faces a certain direction or has a certain view; who remain in the room at all times; who will not allow housekeeping or room service into the room; who eat all their meals in the room, with most either ordered through room service or restaurants that deliver to the room; or who have photo or video equipment out on stands or tripods.

Suspicious behavior for residential renters include paying in cash or with a cashier's check or money order; hooking up just enough household services for someone to stay there; having little or no furniture delivered or set up; establishing no mail service to the house; keeping curtains and shades pulled all the time; not having any lights on at night (photographing through light is very difficult); and never leaving the rental unit except when it correlates to your activities.

Things to be on the lookout for with business rentals include the following: the renter requests windows or doors facing certain directions; the tenants have no office or business equipment, customers, business license, mail service, or business paraphernalia, such as cards or letterheads; the business has few employees; the tenants keep very strange office hours; there is photo or video recording equipment in the office; and the business does no advertising.

When conducting surveillance from a fixed position, surveillance personnel must have a plausible reason for being in the area. This cover for action is limited only to the imagination of the agents, and many unique ruses have been used very effectively. One common ruse is operating as a vendor, which gives the person "cover" to be in the same place for extended periods. In assessing a vendor, you should ask yourself the following questions: Is the vendor's locale reasonable for the business he is trying to conduct? Does the proprietor look more interested in watching your building than in making sales? Do you notice cameras or videos? What hours does the vendor operate, and do those hours coincide with the best time to sell that product? Other common covers are repairing automobiles, selling products door-to-door, fixing utilities, making out in a park, walking a dog, doing construction work, or sitting at a café.

Fixed site surveillance can also be done from vans, utility vehicles, and automobiles. Most threat organizations will use stationary vehicles to conduct their surveillance, since they leave no paper trail, and vehicles and people can be swapped to avoid suspicion. Vans with windows that allow outside observation make good surveillance platforms, but remember that they need a reason to be there. When used, vans should have some type of business logo attached to explain their presence.

Automobiles are usually parked facing away from the target, and the rearview mirrors are used for observation. So instead of being set up for normal operation, these vehicles will be set up differently so that the passengers can use the mirrors to observe your actions. Be watchful for automobiles with passengers who never get out, but rather sit for hours in the same position. Also be on the lookout for bad "shift changes" between surveillance team members. For example, one car has been parked at a certain spot all day; another car drives up and parks the same way or communicates with the first car in some way; then the first vehicle drives away. That's a bad shift change.

Surveillance teams often use women and children, since people will tend to ignore them. Also, children are great at gathering intelligence or watching places and people. As anyone with kids knows, they can repeat their whole day at school or the playground from memory and in great detail, and when asked to find out something specific, they usually do an excellent job. Using kids for surveillance is great for the surveillance team and bad for the target. I have even seen security personnel let children inside a fence line to retrieve a ball. Do not ignore children as a potential threat!

As shown, fixed site surveillance can take place anywhere, but it is especially effective at choke points. Don't forget these when setting up your surveillance-detection plan.

Warning Signs of Fixed Site Surveillance
- People are dressed improperly for an area.
- Work crews have a work vehicle or van but are not doing any work. (Call the city or the company to find out if the workers are supposed to be there and what work is being done.)
- Individuals are observed more than once in an area you have identified as a likely surveillance spot because of its location and areas of observation.
- Vehicles have altered license plates, mud or dirt obscuring part of the number, paint alterations, new logos painted on, or lots of trash in the interior or around the outside.
- Individuals constantly shift their body positions from sitting too long, eat in their vehicle, have photography or other types of recording equipment, or use the bathrooms in local businesses and then return immediately to their vehicle.
- Individuals either get out of the vehicle just so the agents can have a better view of a target, or never get out of their vehicle.
- Individuals turn away or lower their eyes when you or someone from the site under observation looks at them.
- Individuals hang around buildings for no reason or pace in front of entrances.
- Individuals enter or exit a fixed site immediately after the potential target does something (a correlating activity and one of a surveillance team's most common mistakes).
- Individuals read while standing for long periods, or stand around a broken-down vehicle instead of trying to fix it or calling a tow truck.
- A person or group of people are always at the same coffee shop or café, looking at a certain place for an extended time day after day, possibly with cameras, or writing something down or making a phone call when the target passes by.
- One park bench or picnic area never seems to be empty—and it just happens to be the one offering an excellent view of the targeted area. (Remember, it is not what they seem to be doing that matters, but whether they can observe the target.)
- A person periodically comes out of a building, café, or park to the same vehicle and talks with someone in the vehicle, obviously being careful not to block the view of the person in the vehicle, and then returns to the area he came from.

- Lights are on in a room of a building that gives a view of the target when no other rooms of the building are lit, perhaps late at night or early in the morning before typical office hours.
- Curtains or blinds in one area never seem to move, while the other window coverings in the building are opened and closed normally throughout the day.
- Vehicles parked illegally in an area that lets the passengers observe the target or vehicles, and remain in the same spot for extended periods for no apparent reason.
- Vehicles always seem to break down in the same place or area, which happens to offer a great view of the target.
- A vehicle parks, but no passengers get out.

Moving Surveillance

Moving (or en route) surveillance is the most difficult type to conduct. To accomplish it, the terrorist must place individuals or vehicles close to the subject while the latter is moving. There are three forms of en route surveillance: on foot, in a vehicle, and a combination of both.

Foot Surveillance

Foot surveillance may be conducted by one or more individuals. One-person foot surveillance is rather complicated and is fairly easy to detect. The surveillant must remain relatively close to the target, particularly in congested areas, to avoid losing him. Conversely, in less-congested areas the agent can maintain a greater distance, but the lack of other pedestrians makes him more noticeable. Knowing that he is somewhat obvious, he will likely use a disguise or even a series of disguises to vary his appearance. One indicator of the possible use of a disguise is a shopping bag or some other container for a change of clothes, particularly if the bag is from a store not found in the area or it somehow seems out of place. In elevators, the target should watch for individuals who wait for him to push a button before selecting a floor one flight above or below the one he selected.

Two-person foot surveillance is more effective because the second person provides greater flexibility. Normally, one surveillant will remain close to the target while the second stays at a greater distance and may follow the first on the same or the opposite side of the street. Periodically, the two will change positions so that if the target spots one of them, that individual will soon be out of sight, leading the target to think that he was mistaken about being followed. Obviously, spotting this form of surveillance is more complicated, but if the target is alert to the people in his vicinity, he will eventually detect the same surveillants over time.

Foot surveillance with three or more people uses the most sophisticated techniques and is the most difficult to spot. Generally, one agent will remain behind the target close enough to respond to any sudden moves. The second surveillant will stay behind the first on the same side of the street and keep him in sight. A third person will travel on the opposite side of the street parallel with or just behind the target. In areas where the target has few paths to choose from, one surveillant may walk in front of the target, where he is least likely to cause suspicion. The positions of the other surveillants are usually behind the target and are frequently changed, most commonly at intersections. The agent directly behind the target may move to the opposite side of the street, while another surveillant moves in close behind the target. With additional personnel, any surveillant who thinks that he has been observed may drop out of the area by switching positions not only with the surveillants behind him, but also with those across the street and perhaps in front of him.

I briefly covered foot surveillance because it may be evident around your choke points, your primary areas, or while you are moving short distances between locations.

Vehicle Surveillance

Vehicle surveillance is more commonly used against Americans than foot surveillance, primarily because as Americans we are more likely to travel by vehicle than on foot. But some of the characteristics are the same.

Vehicle surveillance requires a high degree of sophistication and training. As with foot surveillance, it may involve one or more operatives, as well as one or multiple vehicles.

At a minimum in a one-person surveillance effort, the person in the vehicle needs a tape recorder. If no radio or cell phone is available, then two people are required in each vehicle: one to drive and one to act as observer/recorder. Single-vehicle surveillance suffers from the same drawbacks as one-person surveillance. However, there are many ploys and tactics that the surveillance team may use to vary their appearance and location. Therefore, if you suspect surveillance, try to remember aspects of those vehicles you find suspicious and that cannot easily be changed, such as the make, model, color, and any apparent body damage (e.g., rust, dents). You should also look at the people driving the vehicles and try to memorize their features. It may be easy to swap a vehicle that has been compromised, but finding trained surveillance personnel is much harder.

Five or six vehicles are normally used, with two or more operators for each vehicle so that if the target parks his vehicle and walks away, the surveillance can be resumed on foot while the driver remains with the vehicle. Using multiple vehicles permits the threat to switch positions or drop out when necessary to reduce the chances of being detected, but it requires that the occupants of the vehicle are able to communicate. One vehicle follows the target vehicle and directs the other vehicles, which may follow the lead surveillance vehicle, precede the target vehicle, or travel on parallel streets. At intersections when the target vehicle is turning, the vehicle following directly behind the target vehicle will generally travel straight ahead while alerting all other vehicles to the new direction of the target vehicle. Another vehicle in the formation will then take a position behind the target vehicle and become the lead vehicle, taking over the responsibili-

ty for giving instructions to the other surveillance personnel. The former lead vehicle then makes a U-turn or travels around the block to take up a new position, ready to resume the lead vehicle position again when necessary during surveillance.

The surveillance vehicles are generally inconspicuous to the area, have no distinguishing marks or bright paint colors, and have four doors. The distance between the target and the surveillance vehicles will vary depending on speed, but the surveillance vehicle driver will try to keep one or two vehicles between him and the target. Sometimes it may be necessary for a surveillance vehicle (especially if there is only one vehicle) to break traffic regulations to avoid losing the target. If you see a vehicle run a red light, make an illegal U-turn, travel over the speed limit, or make dangerous or sudden lane changes in an apparent effort to keep up with you, focus your attention on that vehicle and the people inside.

Potential targets with well-established routines enable the surveillance agents to use methods that are much more difficult to detect. Two examples of moving vehicle surveillance that are hard to detect are leading and progressive surveillance.

During leading vehicular surveillance, the vehicle will travel in front of the target while watching for turns. When the target turns, the observer makes a note of the turn. The next time the target is surveilled, the vehicle in front will turn where the subject previously turned. Over time, the threat will discover the entire route to the target's residence or workplace while still driving in a position that creates much less suspicion and is almost impossible to detect if the target or his security detail is not paying close attention to what is taking place to the front.

Two methods can be used to conduct progressive vehicle surveillance. In the first method, individuals are placed at key intersections along the probable route that the subject will take. When the target turns, the surveillants note this and adjust the positions of the surveillance vehicles along that portion of the route for the next trip. Eventually the threat will discover the entire route, with a minimum chance of compromise by the target or his security team. While providing more security from the threat's point of view, this method is extremely time consuming and manpower intensive for the threat.

The other progressive surveillance method is more common. In this method, the surveillance team will follow the subject in a vehicle. When the subject turns, the surveillance vehicle will continue on and note the turn in his log, so that on the next occasion a surveillance vehicle will already be parked on the street where the target turned previously, ready to pick up the subject. As with leading surveillance, this method eventually uncovers the entire route with minimal chance of compromise, and it involves much less manpower for the threat to succeed.

Because both leading and progressive surveillance efforts are extremely difficult to detect, the target should vary his routine so that a threat cannot use either method against him.

Warning Signs of Moving Surveillance
- A vehicle is going slower than the rest of the vehicles in the surrounding area for that time of day or that location.
- A vehicle's speed is erratic, indicating that the driver's attention is somewhere other than on his driving, perhaps looking at a person or possible target and then becoming aware of his speed and either speeding up or slowing down rapidly to maintain a certain distance.
- A person on a bike or scooter drives by and looks hard at the possible target.
- Two or more people are in a vehicle, and one of them is obviously looking at the target and not at the road or the driver as if having a conversation, which would be normal.
- A lone driver or passenger exhibits quick jerky head movements, as if taking notes or sketching.

- A person walks by doing what seems like a pace count or timing of a gate entrance as it is opening or closing.
- A person appears to be timing the walking speed of the target as he moves by on foot.
- A vehicle starts or stops when the target does, especially motorcycles or scooters that pull over, shadowing the target's car or motorcade but never passes.
- A vehicle passes the target, stops, possibly parks illegally, but no one gets out
- A vehicle is driving too fast or slow for that area and time of day.
- A vehicle makes erratic moves, changing lanes or moving in and out of traffic patterns as if the driver had a place to go, but then abruptly stops in response to the target's movements.
- A vehicle goes through intersections more slowly than normal or rounds a corner slowly, or a driver pokes the nose of his car around a corner and then pulls back like he is peeking.
- A pedestrian or vehicle maintains the same distance from the target even though the target and his security are varying their speed.
- A vehicle ducks behind other vehicles or objects, or a person moves quickly into stores or doorways when the target stops.
- A vehicle or pedestrian is moving on parallel streets at roughly the same speed as the target (you and your security need to be observant of parallel streets when passing by intersections, side streets, or alleys).
- A vehicle hides behind other vehicles in the traffic pattern and pulls out to pass but then drops back, attempting to maintain a certain distance from the target.
- A vehicle pauses in a traffic circle or stays in the traffic circle until the target has exited.
- A pedestrian hesitates or looks around before following the target into a building.
- A person enters or leaves a building just before or after the target or security detail does.

Technical Surveillance

With the recent advances in technology, particularly electronics, the threat has numerous devices readily available to assist the surveillance efforts. These include, but are not limited to, still and video cameras and vehicle tracking devices. LoJack is one such tracking device, but there are many other common devices that work off the local cellular network and also use GPS. If the car you drive has OnStar or another similar service, be aware that in other countries you have no idea who is using the information available from this device and for what purposes. Among other types of surveillance tools are any listening/recording devices and computers, which can be used to identify a prospective target and record his movements and security; infrared paint, which can be seen only through special goggles; scanners or listening devices placed inside the target's vehicle to eavesdrop on the target's security detail or cell phone.

Combination Surveillance

In any high-threat environment in which you consider yourself or your client to be at risk, you can expect a combination of all the surveillance techniques to be employed against you: stationary surveillance at your residence or work site and choke points, vehicular surveillance while you are moving, and electronic surveillance, in which all your activity will be recorded by various technical devices.

Warning Signs of Combination Surveillance

- A person stays at a certain place from which he can observe the target for a long period or stays in one location and then moves to different locations throughout the day, but he remains in the same general location from which he can observe the target.
- A bicyclist stops suddenly, gets off, acts as if he is working on the bike, gets back on and rides farther, and then repeats the same act at different locations, always keeping the target in his area of observation.
- A motorist drives around acting as if he is looking for a parking spot but ignores one if it becomes available.
- Two lovers on the grass in a park across the street seem out of place because of the weather or time of day.
- The wrong type of vehicle is sighted in an area or at a time when it is not usually seen (e.g., using a delivery vehicle during hours when such vehicles do not normally operate).
- Crews are doing work that seems normal except for the location or time of day.
- An otherwise normal road repair is being done after normal working hours or that can't be confirmed by the construction company or city.

VULNERABILITIES OF SURVEILLANCE

While conducting surveillance, the threat has certain vulnerabilities that you can look for and exploit. Remember, the most important thing about conducting surveillance is that the surveillance agents must be able to see the target—you. They have no way to control your environment without giving themselves away, so they have to deal with the day-to-day problems also. As noted earlier, they have to deal with distractions while trying to keep an eye on you and record your movements. Some of the common mistakes that surveillance teams have made in the past include the following:

- The same individuals or vehicles are seen throughout the day at different times/locations.
- The surveillants' demeanor or their type of vehicle doesn't fit the area.
- They have an unusual number of cameras or are taking pictures of things people don't normally photograph.
- They spend an inordinate amount of time talking into a phone, walkie-talkie, or earpiece.

- They have obviously correlated their movement with the target's.
- They pass visual signals to other vehicles or cars.
- They take a lot of notes.
- They seem interested in your movement but quite noticeably avoid any eye contact.
- They spend a lot of time reading newspapers or books, peeking up frequently to observe.
- When following somebody in a vehicle several cars back, they hide directly behind the target vehicle with cars in between, and every once in a while they will pull a little left or right to confirm that the target vehicle is still there.

One thing to do when inspecting your vehicle is to check the taillights, brake lights, and turn signals. Surveillance teams often put red or yellow stickers on these. The stickers are hard to detect, but there will be a little blacked-out spot so that at night the vehicle is much easier to see. Alternately, they will sometimes drill a little hole into the coverings of these lights for the same purpose; at night it's like sending up a little flare with the unfiltered light coming out the hole. The harder your vehicle is to pick out, the closer the surveillance vehicles will have to be, making them easier for you to detect.

One last thing to talk about is the importance of having good communication between you and any countersurveillance personnel you employ. Your countersurveillance personnel should be positioned around the fixed sites and choke points for the best chance of observing surveillance activities and possible site preparation for an attack on you. With effective communication, you can alert them when you are about to approach their area of observation. With this warning, they can start looking for any correlating activities by the threat's operatives as they get into place to begin their surveillance or attack.

While working in Iraq, our security detail sent out a quick reaction force to observe those areas identified as choke points along the routes we traveled. Twice these details noticed activities relating to our approach of the choke point and warned us, allowing us to move to an alternate route and avoid the attacks that were being put into place.

I cannot stress too much the importance of countersurveillance for anyone considered high risk. It should be considered a part of doing business for high-risk facilities to conduct this type of operation daily.

And remember, if you see the same person or vehicle two or more times and the sightings are separated by time, distance, and direction, there is a strong possibility that you are under surveillance.

CHAPTER 8

Your Vehicle

The vehicle you use has to meet several criteria, such as being secure, having the ability to escape a threat, and helping you keep a low profile. When traveling by automobile, you must make yourself a difficult target because, as emphasized, you are most vulnerable while in transit. The harder you make it to distinguish your vehicle from those that the locals drive, the more difficult you make it for terrorists to identify you as an American or a foreigner and the more difficult it is for a surveillance team to locate and follow your vehicle. Whatever you do, avoid obvious symbols of America: Jeeps, Cadillacs, pickup trucks, and sport utility vehicles (SUVs).

Since keeping a low profile is very important to avoid or prevent any attack, you will want to use protective measures that do not draw unnecessary attention to yourself. By being discreet, you make it much harder for the threat to gather any intelligence on you or your activities. With no intelligence available, the threat cannot plan, which makes you a hard target.

Of course, some people have a different point of view and prefer to have very notice-

SUVs can be seen for miles and instantly identify you as a foreigner, most likely an American. Instead, choose a vehicle used by locals.

able protective measures. While obvious protective measures can deter some attacks against you, such as kidnapping, if you are valuable enough as a target, then your enemies will use what they can gather through their surveillance to come up with a plan to counter all your security measures. If they want to kill you, they will take the increased security into consideration when planning. Your low-profile and low-visibility measures thwart attempts to gather actionable intelligence against you. Lack of such intelligence is the threat's weakest link.

Equip whatever type of vehicle you decide to use so that it will handle a crisis long enough for you to reach a safe haven. When choosing a vehicle, remember that rear-wheel drive is more durable, and unibody designs do not stand up to punishment very well. Also, if possible, you want to have an automatic transmission instead of a standard. For evasive driving, a vehicle with an automatic transmission is much easier to handle, and it will make it much easier for a passenger to take control of the vehicle if the driver is disabled.

Bigger isn't always better. These types of vehicles are easy targets for surveillance because they stand out so much, even compared to SUVs, and always draw attention.

ARMOR

Should you drive an armored vehicle? Maybe, but you have to remember that an armored vehicle is capable of sustaining an attack from large-caliber rifles and heavy weapons for only 20 to 25 seconds—it will not make you invulnerable. You must also consider that an armored vehicle could make you stand out, depending on the type, and in some locations just having one could make you a target.

If you decide to go the armored route, there are several ways to do this. First, you could buy a fully armored vehicle from a manufacturing firm, which costs between $80,000 and $200,000. Just remember that factory-armored vehicles may need to be upgraded in the various ways described in this chapter so that performance is adequate for survival driving. Second, you can modify your vehicle with 200 pounds of

armor for approximately $800 to $1,000. This option will provide considerable protection from handguns and the blast effects from small explosives. Third, you can insert either steel or layered aluminum panels in the doors (primarily on the driver's and front passenger's sides). With either type of do-it-yourself reinforcement, you should laminate a panel of Lexan to the side windows. Lexan comes in different levels of thickness; the threat level will determine the thickness you need. Laminate a sheet of Mylar film to the exterior surface of the glass and then insert the window with the glass facing out. You will not be able to open and close the windows, which shouldn't matter since you should *always* drive with windows up. Just make sure the vehicle has a functioning air conditioner and heater. You can also place spare body

An armored sedan is much harder for surveillance to detect and offers all the same protections as an armored SUV.

An armored vehicle that has taken rounds.

armor over the seats and hang it on the doors for protection. Another option for reinforcing floorboards or seats is a "bomb blanket," a Kevlar blanket used by explosive ordnance disposal (EOD) personnel.

If you do not have the ability to upgrade protection for the entire vehicle, at a minimum you should strengthen the driver's-side door and the windshield. The driver is the most important person during movement and needs to be protected—if anything happens to him, the whole vehicle can be stopped.

ENGINE

If attacked, you need to move as quickly out of the kill zone as you can. When you choose a vehicle, you want one that has good acceleration and horsepower. Any good, medium-powered vehicle will have enough power to ram through vehicle barricades. Eight-cylinder engines will react much more quickly and are more powerful. If you choose to modify the vehicle yourself rather than buy an armored vehicle from the factory, make sure the engine has enough horsepower to perform adequately, especially when you need added power.

TIRES

When selecting or upgrading a vehicle, tires are among the most important, yet often neglected items. Make sure you get tires that meet all your needs—for day-to-day, inclement weather, and security driving when necessary. For example, high-performance or high-speed tires are not very good in some environments because of the tread pattern. Do your research and get the right ones for your situation. Never assume that just because the tires came with the vehicle they will do just fine.

Generally, you should choose a radial tire instead of a bias ply; the choice of steel, fiberglass, or Kevlar will probably be based on what is available rather than on what you prefer. If you have specialty tires on your vehicle, make sure you have plenty of spares, since they will not be readily available in many areas.

How Is a Tire Put Together?

A tire is built in layers consisting of the *bead bundle*, which is a loop of high-strength steel cable coated with rubber. This is what gives the tire the necessary strength to stay seated on the wheel rim. Next is the *body*, which is made up of several layers of different fabrics, called *plies*. The most common ply fabric used at this time is polyester cord. The cords in a radial tire run perpendicular to the tread. The plies are coated with rubber to help them bond with the other components and to seal in the air. A tire's strength is often described by the number of plies it has. Most car tires have two body plies. Then there are the *belts*, such as those in steel-belted radial tires. Belts made from steel are used to reinforce the area directly under the tread, providing some resistance to punctures and helping the tire stay flat so it maintains the best contact with the road surface. Tires with higher speed ratings have *cap plies*, which are an extra layer or two of polyester fabric to keep everything in place when spinning at higher speeds. The *sidewall* provides all the lateral stability for the tire and protects the body plies. Finally we have what everyone sees, the *tread*, which is made from a combination of many different kinds of natural and synthetic rubbers. The tread is what has the patterns that give the tire traction; we have all seen tires worn smooth and know how slippery the surface of those tires is.

What Do All Those Numbers and Letters Mean?

Each letter or number on the side of a tire identifies something unique about that tire. There are letters that designate the type of vehicle: P for passenger, LT for light truck, and T for temporary. Tire width is given in millimeters from sidewall to sidewall. The aspect ratio is the height of the tire from the bead to the tread; the smaller this is, the wider the tire is. High-performance tires have a lower aspect ratio than other tires. Tires with a lower aspect ratio provide better lateral stability, which is needed when a car makes a turn because lateral forces are generated and the tire must resist these forces to keep its shape. Tires with a lower profile have shorter, stiffer sidewalls so they resist better. An R tells you the tire is a radial-constructed tire; older tires can have different markings. The rim diameter for the tire is also posted on the side.

Passenger car tires also have a grade on them as part of the uniform tire quality grading (UTQG) system. The tire's UTQG rating tells you three things: treadwear grade, traction grade, and temperature-resistance grade. The treadwear grade comes from testing the tire in controlled conditions on a government test track. The higher the number, the longer you can expect the tread to last. The traction grade is AA, A, B, or C, with AA at the top of the scale. This rating is based on the tire's ability to stop a car on wet concrete and asphalt. It does not indicate the tire's cornering ability. Finally, the temperature-resistance ratings are A, B, and C. This grade is a measure of how well the tire dissipates heat and how well it handles the buildup of heat. The temperature grade applies to a properly inflated tire that is not overloaded. Underinflation, overloading, or excessive speed can lead to more heat buildup, which can cause tires to wear out faster or even fail.

Next we have the service description, which is the load rating, and the speed rating. The load rating is a number that correlates to the maximum rated load for that tire; a higher number indicates that the tire has a higher load capacity. The speed rating is the letter that follows the load rating and indicates the maximum speed allowable for this tire as long as the weight is at or below the rated load.

Somewhere else on the tire will be the number for the tread wear on the tire, with 100 being the test baseline. Any multiple of

The designation P2425/65R17 105H on this tire means:

P = passenger car
245 = tire
65 = aspect ratio
R = radial construction
17 = wheel diameter
105 = 2,039 pounds load index
H = 130 mph maximum speed

The designation LT265/75R16 means:

LT = light truck
265 = tire width
75 = aspect ratio
R = radial construction
16 = wheel diameter

The designation 108/104S means:

108/104 = the load index as established by the Rubber Manufacturers Association, which sets the industry standard
108/104 = 1984/2,005 pounds
S = indicates the tire has a maximum speed of 112 mph

Also on the tire are the tread-wear, traction, and temperature ratings.

this is how long it should last compared to the baseline test.

Next will be the traction rating: either A, B, or C. This is based on a wet-surface braking test. A is the best rating.

Some tires have extra symbols that stand for the load index and speed symbol. The load index is the maximum load capacity that a tire is designed to support under optimal operating conditions. The speed rating and the load index are designated in the laboratory using tires that are in perfect condition on excellent road conditions, with the correct inflation and no wear and tear. The higher the speed rating, the better the handling and maneuverability compared to the lower-speed-rated tires. The ratings are as follows: M, N, P, Q, R, S, T, U, H, V, W, Y, and Z, with M being the lowest rating at 81 mph and Z the highest at 186 mph.

All your spares need to be full size, and they need to be stored so they are easily accessed when they are needed. Pack the spares on top, along with the equipment needed to change them. Whenever you are carrying baggage or other cargo, it goes under the tire-changing equipment. If you lean the spares up against the rear seat during movement, they also provide another layer of protection to the rear.

Tires need to be inspected every time you get into the vehicle. It should be part of your premovement and end-of-day inspections. You are checking for tread depth and proper inflation. When tires become under-inflated, they can separate from the rim during high speeds or extreme maneuvers.

Finally, remember that rubber is a luxury during an incident. If you need to, you can drive forever on the rims—and that's what you should do in a crisis. I have seen people stop during a ramming exercise because they didn't think the car could continue. I got them back on the track, and we rammed two more barricades, completing the exercise with no problems. I have also had to make overseas security details continue a movement on a flat tire because of the high-threat environment; they were worried about hurting the rim or ruining the flat tire. These things should be of no concern as long as the vehicle can still be driven. Don't let a flat tire make you hesitate in a situation. Just control your speed and watch your turns, but keep moving.

SUSPENSION

Your vehicle should have a heavy-duty suspension, which will enable it to drive over terrain (including roadside curbs) that most vehicles can't. If you have upgraded the armor on your vehicle, adding heavy-duty suspension will ensure that you haven't degraded the performance and handling characteristics.

To check out the suspension, drive it over the worst terrain you might possibly have to evade over, including driving over a curb. Get some heavy-duty shock absorbers, and install front and rear anti-sway bars if you don't have them (Roadmaster makes excellent ones). The bars will keep the vehicle from leaning over in a heavy turn, keeping the vehicle's center of gravity over the wheels, where it needs to be.

MIRRORS

Another modification to make your vehicle as secure as possible is to replace the mirrors. Most factory-installed mirrors just meet minimum requirements; you need to go beyond that. Install oversized outside mirrors on both sides of the vehicle to allow for a wider field of view, thus reducing your blind spots. Replace the interior mirror with a larger one or put a mirror in so that the front passenger can use it. Remember, the more you see, the safer you will be.

COMMUNICATIONS EQUIPMENT

Make sure you install a two-way communications system in the vehicle. Yes, I know that cell phones rule, but there are going to be places in both urban and rural environments where cell phones won't get a signal but a good radio will, especially a high-frequency radio.

TINTED WINDOWS

The choice of whether to have tinted windows depends on the type of operations and tactics the threat uses. Tinted windows make it difficult for someone on the outside to look into the interior of the vehicle to see whether the target is in the vehicle and where people sit inside the vehicle. However, tinted windows also make it more difficult to perform a bomb search if one is required because you were forced to park in an area that is not secure.

ALARMS

Alarms are a must. Most come factory installed, but you can buy aftermarket alarms and install them yourself if the vehicle you select doesn't have them. There are many types of alarms on the market that are affordable to everyone. Although alarms can be circumvented and people tend to ignore them, it is an observable deterrent and may make the threat move on to another target on the hit list.

GAS TANK

When working in a high-threat environment, you should have an armored gas tank and one that is self-sealing. It is better to keep the gas tank as full as possible in case you are attacked, since the most explosive thing about a gas tank is the fumes. Never let the tank get less than half full.

BRAKES

You will probably need to improve your braking system if you did not order a vehicle customized for defensive driving. You should install semimetallic brake pads in the front, replace your brake fluid with DOT 4 fluid for better performance, and ensure that your emergency brake will allow bootleg turns. There are several ways to prepare the brake so it will not catch. For hand-pull brakes under the steering wheel, you can use a piece of small PVC pipe or shrink-wrap to cover the teeth so they will not catch. That way you can use it like a regular foot brake. If you can't find a way to do this, then you need to practice your bootleg turn and other evasive maneuvers with the emergency brakes you have.

LOCKS

Install a gas door that locks or put a lock on the current one, even if you have an inside-the-vehicle release. Put a hasp and lock on the hood of the vehicle, and disconnect the automatic trunk release so the key has to be used to open it. Make sure the trunk has a different key than the ignition.

Lock your vehicle papers in a separate container, such as a bank bag, since most vehicle papers have residence or work addresses on them.

KEYS

This is not really a modification to your vehicle to make it safer; it is a behavior modification that will make it and you safer. You and your security must control your keys at all times. If you must leave your car with parking attendants or mechanics, leave only your ignition key, not your house or office keys, which may be duplicated. If possible, leave someone there with the key and start the vehicle when it is required, keeping the keys out of the hands of unknowns.

Valet parking at hotels or other event venues is sometimes mandatory. If you must use valet parking, do not leave your keys with the valet. Ride with the attendant to where your vehicle will be parked, lock the vehicle, and keep the keys with you. This will ensure that you know where the vehicle is located and that you have the keys in your possession if you have to leave in a hurry. It also prevents someone from making an impression of the key or duplicating it.

SAFETY FEATURES

Seat Belts and Air Bags

The driver, the passenger, and security staff all need to keep their seat belts on while the vehicle is moving. Because of the extra equipment they wear, some security detail employees might have to wear seat belt extenders, but seat belts are essential to keep everyone from bouncing around the interior. While traveling in stop-and-go traffic in an urban environment, security personnel can keep their seat belts off if going less than 25 mph to make it easier to exit the vehicle to deal with any problems that might arise. I have worked with some security personnel who refused to wear seat belts even during high-speed travel because they claimed it limited their ability to operate. If your security staffers say this to you, then they are not very well trained—you need to reconsider their employment.

I have talked to personnel and examined their vehicles after enemy contact and IEDs have gone off, and usually about half the bullet holes in the unarmored vehicles were outgoing. This happens when the driver is maneuvering, driving over curbs, braking, and speeding up, and the unsecured security guy is getting thrown around while trying to fire his weapon at an assailant. Or his finger is on the trigger while he is attempting to line up shots, and every jerk and bump causes him to jerk his weapon. This puts everyone in the vehicle at risk and does nothing to stop your attackers. Wearing seat belts has never stopped well-trained security personnel from performing their jobs, and seat belts *do* save lives.

Air bags are a personal choice, but I always pull the fuse in cars I drive because I don't want to have to deal with them in an emergency. Some people feel safer with air bags. This decision needs to be left up to the driver, since it concerns him the most.

Trunk Escape Latch

If your vehicle has a trunk, make sure it has an interior trunk escape latch. Most cars come equipped with them now, but if you get your vehicle overseas it might not. If it doesn't, you can have one installed.

Fire Extinguishers

Have at least two fire extinguishers in the vehicle, one mounted to the frame and one mounted in the trunk. You want them mounted so that during evasive maneuvers they don't go flying or rolling inside the vehicle, which can be very distracting to the driver and others in the vehicle. Remember also that fire extinguishers are for people first and equipment second. Make sure everyone is safe and not on fire, and then worry about the vehicle and other equipment.

First Aid and Survival Kits

Every vehicle needs to be equipped with first aid and survival kits that are geared

Seat belt extenders may be necessary for security agents carrying a lot of bulky equipment or gear.

toward the environments you will be traveling in. Your first aid kit should be equipped to treat major trauma (e.g., a gunshot wound). If possible, have some intravenous therapy equipment and people who know how to use it. The survival kit should also contain water, an alternate means of communication, and money at a minimum. Other items can be added as needed.

Cameras

Always carry a digital camera and/or video camera in the vehicle, or in each vehicle if you are doing convoy operations. When it is necessary for you to give a good description of suspected surveillance or possible attackers, a picture or video will take out all subjectivity and record actual evidence.

Sledgehammers

Mount 5- or 10-pound sledgehammers to the floor in the front and rear seats. These tools can be very important if your vehicle flips onto its top or takes a hard impact—the doors might jam, and armored windows won't roll down. You will need the sledgehammers to pound the windows out so you can exit the vehicle.

MAINTENANCE

You must always keep your car in good mechanical repair, including brakes, headlights, windshield wipers, etc. When you select a vehicle, make sure you pick one that will be easy to maintain and can be worked on by local mechanics. If your primary vehicle goes down, you won't have to wait a week for parts to arrive or someone to be brought in to fix it.

If your vehicle was brought in from out of the country you are working in, you need to tune your vehicle so that it will run on the grade of gasoline or diesel locally available. Most vehicles driven in the United States will run well on local-grade gasoline if the timing is properly adjusted. How do you know when this is necessary? The vehicle will be hard to start, it will ping when you are accelerating, and the engine will continue to run after the ignition is shut off. Adjust the carburetor to the local grade of gasoline; a well-adjusted carburetor will prevent the engine from dying during sudden accelerations and will help provide the most power to the engine. Carburetors should also be adjusted when working at high altitudes to get the most performance out of the engine. (NOTE: Most automobiles sold in the United States after 1980 have electronic fuel injection systems, rather than carburetors, to meet fuel efficiency standards. Adjustments to these vehicles may require the services of a professional. It doesn't matter who does the adjusting, your security team or a professional at a dealership, the important thing is to make sure your vehicles receive regular maintenance. I prefer vehicles that I can adjust myself, so I drive those with carburetors when available.) Vehicles with automatic chokes should be checked to ensure that they are properly adjusted. Improper adjustment will cause a car to stall when the accelerator is pressed to full throttle. You should always let your car warm up to normal operating temperatures before driving to ensure that the choke is fully open.

Check spark plugs, points, and condensers during weekly maintenance. If there is any question about their condition, replace them. Again, many automobiles have electronic ignition systems rather than points and condensers that may require professional adjustments.

Disable the fuel cut-off switch. If this cannot be done, then everyone in the vehicle needs to know the location of the switch and what to do if the switch activates and cuts off fuel to the engine.

One of the most important things to remember is *not to overload your vehicle*. I have seen this happen many times because not enough vehicles were brought to accomplish the mission. Do pretrip planning and make sure you have enough vehicles to do the job. Most people tend to let their hired security element run everything. You need to take an active hand in ensuring that your vehicle is properly chosen, equipped, maintained, and operated—you are the client.

THINGS TO CARRY IN YOUR VEHICLE

- ❏ 2 full-size spare tires
- ❏ 4 cans of Fix-A-Flat
- ❏ Extra tow strap (tow straps should be premounted on all vehicles)
- ❏ Rope
- ❏ Snap links
- ❏ Jack
- ❏ 2 tire blocks
- ❏ 2 or more fire extinguishers
- ❏ Spare hoses and belts
- ❏ Replacement vehicle fluids
- ❏ Water for vehicle and drinking purposes
- ❏ Flashlights/chemical lights
- ❏ Jumper cables
- ❏ Epoxy putty (can be used to repair radiators and oil pans in an emergency)
- ❏ Pry bar for helping to open stuck doors
- ❏ 2 sledgehammers
- ❏ Charger for cell phones and other devices
- ❏ GPS (should be on during movement to track your route)
- ❏ Digital and/or video camera
- ❏ Survival kit
  - ❍ Money in local currency and U.S. dollars
  - ❍ Alternate means of communication
  - ❍ Emergency contact list
  - ❍ Map
  - ❍ Matches
  - ❍ Blankets
  - ❍ Spare clothes
  - ❍ Food
- ❏ First aid kit (A first aid kit in a high-threat environment needs to have items to treat a trauma injury, such as a gunshot.)
  - ❍ Band-Aids of various sizes
  - ❍ Curex bandages
  - ❍ Elastic bandages
  - ❍ Other things to control bleeding (e.g., tourniquet, bungee cords)
  - ❍ Emergency blanket
  - ❍ IVs
  - ❍ Mouth-to-mouth mask
  - ❍ CPR reference card
  - ❍ Aspirin
  - ❍ Specific medications as required

CHAPTER 9

Vehicle Occupant Responsibilities

DRIVER

Driving a vehicle properly is harder than most people think, primarily because they were never taught to drive the vehicle correctly to begin with, just how to operate it as a mechanical device. The driver—no matter who it is (you, a security man, or a hired chauffeur) or how familiar he is with the area—should remain alert at all times and concentrate exclusively on the responsibilities of operating the vehicle.

The driver's only responsibilities are to maintain control of the vehicle no matter what situation it is placed in and to keep the occupants safe. Until the vehicle is forced to come to a complete halt and becomes unmovable, the driver should not use a gun, a radio, a cell phone, or any other device; he should concentrate on keeping the vehicle moving away from the threat. When a situation develops that needs immediate attention, you want the driver to be able to respond. His decisions and how he acts and reacts to the environment around the vehicle could have a direct influence on the lives of all the passengers, especially in a high-threat environment.

Another important but sometimes unrealized requirement for a driver is the understanding that damaging the vehicle for security or defensive reasons is not just okay, *it is expected*. In most cases, the vehicle can and will serve as a weapon against another vehicle or person and is your primary means of escaping the attack. You don't want your driver to be scared to hit or drive over something because he doesn't want to pay for the damage, so make sure he understands that in advance.

The driver should have some type of training in security and defensive driving, as well as practical experience for the region in which he will be working. He also needs the opportunity to practice these skills regularly on every vehicle he will be expected to drive. This book is an excellent tool, but it is not the only training you or your driver should have. There are many schools that offer classes in defensive/antiterrorist driving.

The person driving the vehicle should always maintain a cautious (and careful) attitude and be familiar with the levels of alertness; he should always be at Condition Yellow. As soon as the vehicle car bomb search and vehicle safety check have been completed (see Chapter 15 for specific instructions), the driver should start the vehicle and lock the door. Starting the vehicle allows the driver to know where the keys are, and he can drive away immediately if necessary. Locking the door prevents the driver from being pulled from the vehicle, someone from opening the door and throwing something inside, or someone from entering the vehicle ahead of his passengers or at the same time.

Once the vehicle is started and the door locked, the driver adjusts the seat, seat belt, mirrors, etc. This prepares him for a crisis if it develops, and he can leave immediately when the person he is driving shows up.

Depending on where he is picking up his passengers, the driver should unlock only one door at a time, and people should enter on one side only. As people are entering the vehicle, the driver's door should remain locked, and the driver should have a sidearm out and ready to use in case an unauthorized person attempts to enter the vehicle.

The driver should know the route analysis and the identified choke points and danger areas. While driving, he should be watching several blocks ahead to see what is happening; the farther up he can see, the more quickly he can respond. He also should be *visualizing* two or three blocks ahead; as he approaches each choke point and danger area, he should be going over the preplanned crisis response, preparing to react to an attack if necessary.

If you will be using a hired chauffeur rather than you or your regular security personnel being at the wheel, you must check the person out carefully. If overseas, you should have all prospective drivers vetted with the embassy or some other major company's security staff, someone who can be trusted. Food for thought: if your driver lives in the local economy—can he be trusted? Does an American or other expatriate company have the ability to do good background checks on locals? Not very trustworthy ones. If your driver is a local who has been hired for this job by your company or security detail, he should not be from nor live in the local area you will be working in. There are too many chances for him to pass or let slip information that

could endanger your security. Also if he is not from the local area and has limited contact with locals, this will lessen his chances of being blackmailed by people making threats against him or his family.

Don't use a hired chauffeur unless you have to; if you must, make sure he is qualified and trained in defensive/evasive driving. Remember, your life will depend on how he acts and reacts.

Your driver must follow some basic rules regardless of who he is or how well he is trained. He must remain with the vehicle at all times—he is there to make sure the vehicle is safe for you. While he is waiting for you, do not allow him to stay in the vehicle, which limits his area of view and presents too many distractions. Instruct the driver to stand outside the car to the rear; this gives him the greatest field of view, and he can see if anyone tries to tamper with the vehicle. The driver should not be on his cell phone or walkie-talkie conducting personal business (unless he is part of the larger security detail and uses the phone or walkie-talkie to coordinate movement). This distracts him from his primary job, and you never know to whom he is talking or why. If you come out of your building and the driver is not at the vehicle, *do not approach the vehicle*. As soon as you notice his absence, turn around and move back into the safe area you just left.

Make sure your driver and you have a prearranged signal that will indicate whether it is unsafe to approach the vehicle. This signal can be anything that can be observed from a distance, such as the driver taking his hat off or putting it on, positioning his sunglasses on the left side of his jacket or on his head, or leaning against the vehicle with his arms crossed. This signal is so you will know if someone has captured your driver and is waiting for you to approach the vehicle. Having prearranged signals might not work if the terrorists have blackmailed or recruited the driver. So before approaching your vehicle, always observe the area around your vehicle at least 10 minutes before you leave the security of the building, continue to scan the area for anything suspicious as you approach the vehicle, and look inside the vehicle before opening a door.

You don't need to give your itinerary for the day to the driver; you can tell him where he needs to go and what route to take if he is not your regular driver or part of your security staff.

If your driver is being sent for the day only, you need to give him only a general idea of when to show up at your home (e.g., 0600, even though you don't plan to leave until 0630 or 0700) and never give him the destination in advance. This way you will not be time and place predictable. Once you give that type of information out, you never know who will get it and what they will do with it. This is why, again, you do not want your driver talking on a cell phone or communicating with people, especially if you don't speak his language.

If another driver is substituted without your knowledge for your usual driver, never get into the vehicle until you have checked his credentials with whoever provided him. When checking out the new driver, make sure the person you are talking to on the phone is someone you know personally. Get the substitute's name, license number, and physical description, and give them to the person who is verifying the substitution. Just because Bob was supposed to show up doesn't mean *he* did.

Whenever someone else is driving you, you need to ascertain his level of security awareness, type of training, and experience. This will allow you to determine whether your driving capabilities, security awareness, and alertness are as good as your chauffeur's. If you are better trained and more knowledgeable and understand the threat better than your driver, dismiss him and drive yourself. Contract drivers and chauffeurs have been known to lie about their capabilities and general threat awareness and then freeze up when an attack occurs. This has often led directly to their principals being captured or assassinated.

If you must use a taxi or shuttle van, never give your real destination over the phone. Once again, you do not know who is getting that information on the other end and what they will do with it. Give the correct destination after you get into the cab, and ask the driver not to get on the radio or telephone to report the change. When possible, let the hotel or building you are staying in make the call, so the threat cannot identify you as a possible target by identifying you as a foreigner over the phone.

PASSENGERS

If you have a driver, you are a passenger, and as a passenger you are part of the overall security environment of the vehicle. This means you need to stay mentally alert at all times and be in Condition Yellow while moving. This is not the time to review reports, read the newspaper, make phone calls, or eat your breakfast. A small mirror attached to the passenger's visor can help you observe the rear, since the driver will be occupied with operating the vehicle. You also need to watch the areas that the driver and other security personnel cannot see. Use the extra set of eyes to spot any unusual activity. Make the others aware of anything suspicious, especially to the sides and rear outside their normal field of vision. Remember, as emphasized earlier, the more you see, the safer you will be.

If you are the passenger in a company vehicle or one on loan from someone else, then you should be the one to determine your routes. As emphasized throughout this book, you will need to constantly vary your routes, routines, and departure and arrival times to avoid being predictable by time and place. If you have security personnel working for you, they will determine these for you, but even as a passenger with a security detail you need to know the route, what safe havens are on it, and landmarks along the route. When you did your route analysis, you looked for and identified at least three different routes to and from work, home, and other primary areas. Do not allow yourself to fall into a routine of always taking the same route every day because your driver or your security detail is lazy or unprepared or does not believe in the threat. *Having a routine that makes you time and place predictable can get you killed.*

CHAPTER 10

Driving Basics

Many people consider themselves to be great drivers, but a look at the number of accidents annually in the United States would make you think that no one really knows how to drive—and you wouldn't be completely wrong. Most people are taught how to operate a vehicle as a mechanical device, not to understand the dynamics of driving, the mechanics of the vehicle, and the principles involved. People never admit their own driving deficiencies, and most will say that "there is not a thing you could teach me about driving—I have been doing it since I was 16."

Driving a car is difficult enough in the United States, where there are traffic laws and controlled conditions. When you are living in another country or a high-threat environment where it can be every man for himself, the difficulty of escaping an attack zone or avoiding an overrun attack rises significantly. In this chapter I am going to discuss some things that will improve your driving skills and thereby enhance your chances of survival when moving by vehicle.

SAFETY CHECK

The first thing you need to do is conduct a predriving safety check. If you perform this check every time you get ready to drive a vehicle, it will get easier with time, and it helps develop a few "positive habits" that will increase your overall driving safety.

One of the most important but often-neglected habits you need to develop is very quick and simple: before entering the vehicle, walk around it and look at it carefully. You are looking at the overall condition of the vehicle and whether it is safe to drive.

- Do the tires look OK?
- Do the headlights and turn signals function?
- Do the brake lights work?
- Does the vehicle look level?
- Are there fluid spots or puddles underneath the vehicle?
- Are things hanging underneath the vehicle, which could indicate a possible malfunction?
- Are there any signs of tampering or any objects that have been placed on, in, or around your vehicle by someone intent on harming its occupants?

During the inspection, ensure that all the vehicle's windows are coated with Rain-X, and check to be sure that you have extra radiator fluid, a patch kit, an epoxy kit, and tire sealer/inflator for all four tires. Check your spare tires; you should have at least two easily accessible, full-size spares.

As you get situated inside the car, as the driver you need to be able to "feel" and "listen" to the vehicle as it provides information to you. To do this, you have to sit correctly and hold the wheel correctly. You need to sit with your hips back in the seat and your shoulder blades against the back of the seat. You should never have to lean forward to steer or control the pedals. This means sitting upright in the vehicle, not rigid and unable to flex or move at all.

The seat should be far enough back so you can touch the complete wheel and rotate your right foot between the gas and brake pedals. Keep the heel of the right foot planted on the floor in front of the brake pedal, allowing your foot to rotate between the gas and brake pedals. You must find the correct placement of your heel through trial and error, since everyone's foot size is different. Use the balls of the feet to manipulate the pedals and the toes to make fine adjustments.

One way to get the seating distance right is to sit in the vehicle with the hips back, shoulder blades against the back of the seat, and drape your hands over the steering wheel, with the arms straight. Your wrists should be just at the top of the steering wheel, with the hands hanging over the back. This should give the right distance to allow your hands to move over the whole steering wheel and for foot-control operation, with the knees slightly flexed. Grasping the steering wheel with the hands will keep the arms flexed at the elbows. Make sure your elbows are away from the body.

Once you find your position, lock the seat in and adjust the seat belt. You need to keep your left leg planted on the floor. In SUVs and vans you can plant it against the floor and apply side pressure against the driver's door with your knee for more stability. Your left leg will be used only to apply pressure to the floorboard to help maintain proper body alignment during vehicle weight transfers, especially at higher speeds or during sharper than normal turns.

Not only does the seat belt protect you in case of an accident, as discussed earlier, but it has another function that most people never consider: keeping your hips back in the seat and your butt in place when driving. When you drive over curbs, hit potholes, go into spins, etc., it hard to control steering and pedal action without a stable platform. If you're sliding all over the seat, your input to the steering will be sliding as well, and you will not be able to modulate pressure on the pedals.

Once you have fastened your seat belt properly, you adjust all the mirrors you use, the rearview and two side mirrors, so you can see as much out of all three as possible. The rearview is just like it sounds—it allows the driver to look to the rear—and most drivers adjust it automatically. But the side mirrors are just as important, though frequently ignored by drivers. They should be adjusted so you cannot see the side of your vehicle to lessen the blind spot that most people have in the mirrors. Most people tend to limit the role of mirrors in driving, which is a shame. Mirrors give you a much wider view of your environment.

Now that you have everything set, are you ready to go? First let's talk about the three types of actions (or "inputs") necessary for the driver to control the vehicle: steering, braking, and accelerating.

STEERING

So what does the steering wheel do? Well, most people think the steering wheel is what turns your vehicle and points it in the direction you want it to go. That's the *effect* of the steering wheel, but it is not what it does. The steering wheel just aims your front wheels in the direction you want to go; it does not turn your vehicle. The rolling of the front tires is what causes your vehicle to turn. If you turn the steering wheel with the car sitting still, does it turn? No! But with a little forward movement, it will start to turn, and the faster you go, the faster the turn.

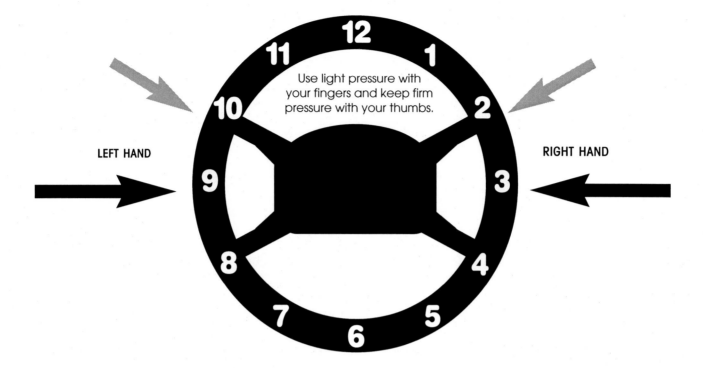

Use light pressure with your fingers and keep firm pressure with your thumbs.

LEFT HAND

RIGHT HAND

Always try to keep your hands at the top part of the steering wheel. This gives you greater freedom of movement.

Turning the vehicle also causes a weight transfer. When you turn to the right, the weight shifts to the left; when you turn left, the weight shifts to the right. The steering wheel is one of the primary means of input into the vehicle. How you hold it will help you read what the vehicle is doing and what you need to do to either counter it or help it. You need to keep your hands at either the 3 and 9 o'clock positions or the 2 and 10 o'clock positions, basically at shoulder height. From this position you can move the wheel the farthest and the fastest it can turn.

Always try to keep your hands at the top part of the steering wheel. This gives you greater freedom of movement.

Shuffle Steering
Shuffle steering enables you to move your hands over the entire wheel without having to cross them. It's the best and smoothest way to steer the vehicle, but it

takes lots of practice. Keep your hands on each side of the wheel at shoulder height or at the 2 and 10 or 3 and 9 positions. You never cross your hands. Your hands will meet at the 12 or 6 position but will not go past this. They stay on their side of the steering wheel. What you are going to do is pull the wheel in the direction you want it to go, since it is smoother to pull than to push. This gives you a nice, smooth input into the steering of the vehicle.

For example, you want to turn left. Since you can see a left turn coming up, you place your left hand at the 12 o'clock position, holding the wheel steady with your right. When you are ready to turn, pull the wheel to the left, allowing it to move freely through the right. If it is a sharp turn and you need to turn the steering wheel more to the left, hold it in place with the right, move your left hand back to the top of the wheel, and pull again until you can complete the turn. When you are ready to get the wheels back to neutral, pull with the right hand, allowing it to pass freely through the left and repeating until the wheels are in the neutral position again.

You do not want to cross your hands. If you are excited and your adrenaline is flowing, you might get your arms and hands tangled and be unable to do the necessary steering; or, just as bad, both of your hands will end up on one side of the wheel and to turn back you have to jerk the wheel all the way around. Also you do not want to "gorilla-grip" the wheel, which means never letting go or moving your hands, because eventually you are going to reach the end of how far you can turn and your hands will be crossed. That means you will need to release, grab the wheel, and probably jerk it, which you are trying to avoid. Smooth steering is best, especially when moving at high rates of speed or making sharp turns. When you are finished with your turn, move your hands back to the neutral position (about shoulder height, at the 2 and 10 or 3 and 9 positions).

Smooth input into the vehicle equals better control. The front of the vehicle will always be able to outmaneuver the rear of the vehicle. We have all fishtailed, or slid the back of our vehicles, without meaning to, by panicking a little and jerking the steering wheel. When you jerk the steering wheel, the front wheels will make the turn. Since a vehicle is designed to stay in a line and turn as a unit, the rear of the vehicle will try to catch up to the front. This causes the rear tires to break their contact patch with the road and lose traction, causing them to slide and you to lose control. When you are being pursued or running from an attack, you need to move as quickly as possible in a controlled manner so that you don't lose precious time trying to regain control, thereby allowing the threat to get closer. Smooth steering will ultimately make you faster.

Eye Movement and Steering

When we talk about steering, we also have to talk about eye movement. This is one of the least talked about but most important aspects of driving. Our entire lives we have learned hand-eye coordination. We train our bodies to follow our eyes and use this every day, when picking up, throwing, or catching things. Driving is no different: wherever our eyes go, that is where our hands will take the vehicle we are driving.

You see examples of this every day when you drive. Have you ever looked at your radio dial to adjust it and when you look up you have drifted over? Or looked at someone or something on the side of the road and drift toward it? Had an animal run in front of your car and you think you are steering away from it but you hit it? Seen an accident where the vehicle hit the only telephone pole, mailbox, or other car on the entire street? These are all examples of a driver moving his eyes to an object and his hands steering toward it.

When driving, you need to keep your eyes up, looking ahead. The sooner you see something, the sooner you can begin your reaction to it. Plus, it allows you to notice the traffic patterns of the cars in front of you. When any type of incident, accident, or attack takes place in front of you, you need to move your eyes to the area you want to go, which is the safest unobstructed area that will allow you to pass or stop without becoming a victim and that causes little or no damage to your vehicle. Believe me, this is not as easy as it sounds and will take lots of practice, because people always want to look at what is going on. But it will make you a much better driver—and keep you alive.

BRAKING

Braking is one of the other actions you control when driving a vehicle. When braking, you want to avoid panic braking, which is when you stomp the pedal to the floor. This is a major muscle movement. If you keep the heel of your foot planted on the floor and rotate it between the gas and brake pedals, and use your toes to modulate the pedals, you take that major leg muscle out of play and you have more control over the input.

You also want to avoid unnecessary braking, one of the leading causes of drivers' losing control during a crisis. People brake unnecessarily because they do not understand what brakes do.

So what do brakes do? Well, for starters, brakes do not stop your vehicle. They only stop the wheels on the vehicle. Your tires, which are mounted on your wheels, are what stop the vehicle. Brakes can also stop your vehicle wheels from turning without stopping the vehicle itself. When you go to 100 percent brakes—i.e., panic braking mode—your wheels lock, and since it is the same patch of rubber on the pavement, it gets hot and starts to slide. This is not a good thing, especially when you realize that if you have 100 percent of your brakes applied, you have 0 percent steering. We have all seen this in action—when you are panic braking to avoid a collision and you start turning the steering wheel as far as you can and the car just does not turn in any direction. It continues going straight, so you keep turning the wheel and then you let off the brakes, and the car suddenly shoots off into the direction the wheels are turned. That's what causes the phenomenon of the brakes canceling out the steering.

So what happens to the vehicle when you apply brakes? Well, the wheels slow down or stop, depending on how much pressure you apply; the car wants to continue traveling straight, so it transfers the weight of the vehicle to the front of the vehicle. This will cause the front of the vehicle to dive down a little and the rear end to lighten up proportionally to the amount of weight transferred.

ABS vs. Threshold Brakes

So how do you want to use the brakes? Well, we want to use controlled braking, and there are two ways to accomplish this: an antilock brake system (ABS) and threshold braking. ABS allows you to push the brake pedal all the way down and not have the wheels lock up. What the computer in ABS does is automatically turn brakes on and off; it senses when the brakes are locked and releases them enough for the tire to rotate and then locks them up again. This will cause the pedal to pulsate or push back against your foot. ABS is so important because it allows you to have some steering control while applying maximum traction to the road surface.

Threshold, or controlled, braking is a better system, but ABS is much more efficient on wet or slippery surfaces for untrained drivers. Threshold braking is something you have to learn, because the driver, not the ABS computer, manipulates the brake pedal. Threshold braking keeps your tires rolling and gives maximum traction, which is your maximum braking capability. You have maximum traction when the tire is skidding approximately 15 percent and rolling 85 percent, which presents enough new rubber to the roadway surface to prevent the tire from melting. With the rolling of the front tire, you have steering control and can turn the wheels to avoid a collision.

How do you achieve threshold braking? You must apply brakes just to the point of lockup. Remember to use the toes of your right foot on the pedal, keeping the heel of your foot on the floor. This takes away your ability to use those major leg muscles, which are harder to control. Apply brake pressure; if your tires lock up, release just enough pressure to let them roll again. You will be able to tell when this is necessary by the sound the tires make—instead of the screech of sliding they will make a chirping sound. You can also tell by the feel on the steering wheel; if you are at the threshold brake point, you will have steering capability. Threshold braking takes practice to read correctly and can be done with ABS on a vehicle when you get more experienced at it.

ACCELERATING

The final driving action I am going to talk about is accelerating. Applying gas to the vehicle is another way of controlling the vehicle and shifting its weight. When you apply pressure to the gas pedal, you are putting more gas into the engine, which causes the car to accelerate. When you accelerate the vehicle, you cause a weight transfer just as you did in steering and braking. Only this time the weight of the vehicle will shift to the rear of the vehicle, which takes the weight off the front, just the opposite of what braking does.

Pedalwork

The last thing I want to talk about in connection with braking and accelerating is using both feet to control the two pedals versus using just the right foot. If you use both feet at once, then any time you save by being able to apply pressure to the two pedals is minimal. But what does increase is the chance of your applying input to the two pedals at the same time. By stepping on the gas and the brake, you are basically canceling each input out. But in times of high stress or panic, it can be a very real reaction. So, in my opinion, it is always better to use one foot to control input into both brake and gas pedals and keep your left foot flat on the floor and braced against the side of the vehicle to help with stability.

AVOIDING ACCIDENTS

Driving is one the most dangerous undertakings that the average person will do in his lifetime. Tens of thousands of accidents happen every year in the United States alone, where we have driving laws and an enforcement capability. Imagine what driving is like in a country where there are no laws and anyone can drive at anytime, regardless of road or vehicle conditions!

Automobiles have become the primary means of transportation throughout the world, and more and more people are driving them. In fact, many people now consider the vehicle they drive their office on wheels. Because we spend so much time in our vehicles in a fairly safe and routine environment, we have a tendency to become complacent about operating the vehicle. Every day you can see people driving while talking on a cell phone, eating or drinking, putting on makeup, shaving, and many other actions that divert their attention from the road.

A lot of multiple-car accidents could be avoided if either driver took the correct action when it was needed. Even if you can't avoid an accident entirely, you might be able to lessen the severity of the impact to your own and the other vehicle by observing what is taking place around you. Noticing vehicles and their drivers and what they are doing will allow you to anticipate that vehicle's course. By watching several cars ahead and tracking the wheels of vehicles in relation to their lane of travel, you can see a person making an unsignaled lane change or turn. Simply observe the distance between the wheel and the lane marker decrease. Most people who are getting ready to change lanes will quickly glance at their mirror or over their shoulder. When you observe this happening, you know that person is going to change lanes, and you can prepare for it.

Observing what is taking place around you just takes practice and can be done whenever you are in a vehicle as either the passenger or driver. The more you practice this, the sooner it will become a habit.

Driving Triangle

Most accidents can be broken down into three major causes: being struck by another vehicle or object; your hitting some vehicle or object, and skidding. The ability to avoid these accidents does not depend solely on your ability to control the vehicle, but also on your ability to understand all three factors that affect the vehicle you are traveling in:

- The vehicle itself
- The environment you are driving in
- The operator of the vehicle

These three factors are called the driving triangle, and when an accident occurs it is because of a failure in at least one of them.

The Vehicle

Through constant research, testing, and after-action reviews of accidents that have taken place, the automotive industry tries to provide the safest vehicles possible for use on the road. What you need to remember, however, is that no matter what the make, model, or price of the vehicle, it is still only a machine, and like all machines it has built-in limitations. These limitations can be aggravated when the vehicle is kept in poor operating condition. Accidents for which the sole cause was outright mechanical failure are uncommon, but a mechanical failure or defect that affects performance can always be a contributing factor.

The Driving Environment

The United States has some of the best-designed, best-maintained, and best-constructed highway systems in the world. But these roads are not immune to the effects of weather and heavy use. When rain, sleet, snow, heat, or other forces of nature have damaged the surface of the road, then it is up to the driver and machine portions of the driving triangle to cope with conditions. In some cases the surface has so deteriorated that the driver/machine combination cannot compensate, and the vehicle becomes less controllable.

The Driver

The third leg of the driving triangle is the only part that is truly flexible and has the ability to adapt to these changes. The driver is responsible for successful implementation of the vehicle-environment relationship.

Accidents are not always "accidental." They take place when an unexpected event occurs, causing a breakdown in the driving triangle. By investigating the accident, it is possible to determine the cause. One of the hardest things to do is getting drivers to accept that the accident was caused by their error. Drivers involved in accidents usually talk about the accidents as though they were nowhere near the accidents when they took place. This happens because most people tend to be overconfident in their driving ability because of their past driving records. How many times have you heard someone say, "I have never had an accident before"?

A majority of people do not have the ability to recognize a dangerous situation because, first, they have never encountered one. Second, they do not understand the capabilities of the vehicle they are driving because they have never tested its capabilities and will probably drive a new vehicle just like they did their last vehicle, even though the handling characteristics are completely different. Third, they have no other training besides basic driver's education, which is how to operate the vehicle for nonemergency situations, or they have never encountered an emergency situation, so basically they do not know how to operate the controls of their vehicle in an emergency or how their body will react.

One of the biggest obstacles most people have is that they don't realize how little they know about cars. How many times have you laughed at stories about people who couldn't find the gas tank or didn't know what the oil light was for? A vehicle is exactly like a computer: they are both inanimate objects until someone tells them what to do by providing input. People even have a tendency to talk about computers and cars in the same way. For example, they will say, "The computer made a mistake," which of course is not true since computers do not make mistakes; the operator makes mistake when he is providing input. So when people claim that their vehicle "lost control," it is again operator error.

There are two basic explanations for loss of control of your vehicle. The first is not so much that you lost control but that you have sloppy driving habits. How many times have you struck the curb or something else while simply trying to back out of the driveway? Or hit, or almost hit, a vehicle in a large parking lot because you simply did not see it until the last second? This doesn't mean the vehicle lost control; it means that while you were operating the vehicle, you were just along for the ride, letting the vehicle do what it wanted and not paying enough attention to your surroundings.

The second type of loss of control is when you are physically out of control. This means just what you would imagine: your heart is pounding, your eyes are bulging, your palms and forehead are sweating, your mouth is dry, and your stomach is in a knot. The only thing you can think of is, "Oh, my God!" When this happens, you have absolutely no control over anything, including yourself or the vehicle, and that vehicle is going wherever the laws of physics take it. This is truly being out of control.

Is there anything you can do when you are plunged into that emergency situation to lessen the damage? Of course, there are several ways to minimize the severity of any accident or impact.

- Always dodge away from oncoming traffic, which in most instances will be to the right unless you are in a country where they drive on the opposite side of the road (e.g., the United Kingdom, Commonwealth countries, and former British colonies, such as Kenya).
- Always drive off the road rather than letting your vehicle skid or slide off. This

This armored vehicle survived a hit by an IED, but the driver could not recover control and it rolled four times.

way you have the chance to pick your own path and, hopefully, miss any large objects, such as trees, signs, or boulders.

- If you have a choice, always aim for a soft target rather than a hard one. For example, pick the collapsible rail before the tree, or a dirt embankment before a boulder.
- If you have to hit something stationary, attempt to hit it a glancing blow so you will slide along its surface. Try to avoid hitting anything head-on.
- Always hit something stationary before you hit something that is moving toward you under its own power. A moving object will combine its energy with yours, thus increasing the force of the impact.
- Keep your wheels rolling, not locked in a skid or slide. This gives you the ability to turn the vehicle.
- Look at where you want to go, not at what you don't want to hit. Remember to move your eyes to the safe area; the vehicle will always go to where you look.

Skids

We talked earlier about skids being one of the major reasons that drivers lose control of a vehicle. The loss of control usually occurs because the driver does not understand what is taking place.

What is a skid? To understand that, you have to understand the three types of friction associated with driving. Friction is the grip between the tires of the vehicle and the road surface; it is what allows us to control the movement of the vehicle (e.g., turning, stopping, starting). There are normally two types of friction at work in a vehicle, static (also known as *stiction*) and rolling. Static friction is when two surfaces are not moving relative to one another (e.g., a tire at rest on a road). Rolling friction is when one surface (a tire) moves relative to another (a road). When a car starts to slide, then a third type of friction comes into play, sliding. There is more of a grip between a stationary wheel and the road than between a sliding wheel and the road.

Once you grasp the concept of the three types of friction, you understand that friction is not a constant when you drive, but rather is always changing. For example, when you increase speed, you lessen the friction between your tires and the road surface. Since friction between the tire and the road is what keeps the vehicle going in the direction you want, a skid occurs when you don't have sufficient friction for an action you have taken with the vehicle.

Cars don't decide to skid on their own; the driver makes that decision by some action he takes. When turning a corner, the outside or loaded wheels are most important for controlling the vehicle. So if you are driving through a changing environment (e.g., snow, rain, sleet, ice), then the vehicle is more likely to skid when the loaded wheels hits these spots than if the inside or unloaded wheels hit that spot. One of the things you need to do when operating a vehicle is to be constantly "feeling" and "reading" the road surface to determine its changing condition and how it will affect your operation of the vehicle. For our purposes, we are going to concentrate on skids caused by four things: braking, accelerating, cornering, and hydroplaning.

Braking Skids

Braking skids are a result of heavy braking, which causes the wheels to lock up. There are essentially three types of braking skids: front-wheel, rear-wheel, and four-wheel (or all wheel).

FRONT-WHEEL BRAKING SKID

This occurs when your front wheels lock up before your rear wheels, causing you to travel in the same direction you were going when you hit your brakes. When this happens, the vehicle cannot be steered. This skid can be caused by having the front brakes set tighter than the rear brakes or by stomping on the brakes. You can make the problem worse by continuing to steer when there is no response.

What to do: First you need to get off the brake and the gas pedals to get some rolling friction established. The car will come back on line if you do this. If you tried to steer the vehicle when it was not responding, all those movements are going to happen at once to the vehicle when you get rolling friction again. Be prepared. Once you have steering back, if the rear wheels start to slide, countersteer until the vehicle is traveling in the direction you want.

REAR-WHEEL BRAKING SKID

This occurs when the rear wheels lock before the front wheels. Since the rear wheels have less traction, when they start sliding they can go just as easily in any direction. So as soon as the car turns slightly, the rear wheels will whip it around 180 degrees from its initial direction of travel. The principal cause of this is the weight being transferred to the front of the vehicle.

What to do: Get off the pedals so the rear wheels can establish some rolling friction. You might need to countersteer in the direction of the skid to help you gain control and get the vehicle moving in the direction you want it to go.

FOUR-WHEEL BRAKING SKID

This is the most common braking skid and the one people are most familiar with because everyone has done it. Panic braking, or applying the brakes too hard, causes this. You lose traction, and away you go. You immediately lose steering capability, but the recovery is easy.

What to do: Get off the brakes so you can regain rolling friction and control. This sounds easy, but it might not be, depending on what is going on. Remember, this is panic braking—you are trying to stop the vehicle at any cost. Never allow panic to control your actions in a vehicle.

Acceleration Skids

Acceleration skids are a result of the driver's input. They are caused by heavy acceleration when the tires spin, causing them to lose traction. This can happen with either rear-wheel-drive or front-wheel-drive vehicles. The acceleration causes the weight to shift to the rear.

POWER SKID OR SPINOUT

This happens when you get a "lead foot," accelerating too fast for road conditions. Too much power to the wheels too quickly will cause the rear tires to lose traction, making them spin. The front tires now act as a pivot point for the vehicle because your side momentum is greater at the rear. When it has no traction, the vehicle can slip and slide all over the place, depending on what it was doing. For example, if the car is cornering a turn when it loses traction, the rear end will whip around.

What to do: Get off all the pedals and countersteer. However, if you feel that the car is going to whip around despite your best efforts at countersteering, you need to lock up all four wheels. *This has to be done before you get to your first spin.* What this does is use the momentum of the vehicle to force the vehicle to slide in the direction the vehicle was moving when you applied the brakes. Practice both techniques; depending on your situation, you might have to use either one.

Cornering Skids

When in a turn at a speed great enough to cause the tires to lose their rolling friction, you exceed the critical speed of curve, which means the tires are rolling and sliding at same time. When this occurs with the rear tires, it's called *oversteer* (sideslip yaw).

What to do: To correct an oversteer, you need to countersteer. That means you need to turn the steering wheel in the direction of the skid and slow the vehicle. *Do not apply brakes while the rear of the vehicle is sliding.* If that happens, then the rear tires will break loose completely, and you will be spinning. If you just take your foot off the accelerator when you feel the rear wheels break loose, the vehicle will regain rolling traction quickly. Be ready to countersteer, but remember not to overcorrect as you do this.

Understeering occurs when the front tires lose their traction.

What to do: This is very simple. Just take your foot off the accelerator, and the vehicle will move back into line for you, regaining

SKID RECOVERIES	
Braking skids	Release brake and attempt threshold braking. Look and steer into the direction you wish to go and keep off the gas.
Acceleration skids	Let off the gas, allowing the tires to regain their traction. Look and steer into the direction you wish to go.
Cornering skids	Get off the brake when it is oversteer; get off the gas when it is understeer. Look and steer into the direction you wish to go.
Hydroplaning	Reduce speed, stay off brakes and gas, look and steer into the direction you wish to go, and be cautious of secondary skids.

traction. But be ready for this especially with front-wheel drive. The vehicle could jump, depending on how much steering you tried before your front tires slowed down enough to gain traction.

Hydroplaning

This type of skid occurs when there is water on the road surface, and the water cannot get out from underneath the tires fast enough. While the vehicle is moving, traction is lost because the tire floats up on a film of water. So now your vehicle is traveling on water instead of a hard surface, and you have no control because you have no friction between the roadway and the tire. Front wheels are usually affected first, so you will lose your ability to steer. This can occur at any speed when the depth of the water exceeds the depth of the tread, but commonly occurs at speeds from 35 to 60 mph. Tires play a big role in this: worn tires means less tread depth, and underinflation will also increase the chances of hydroplaning.

What to do: The best way to prevent hydroplaning is having good tires and to keep your tire pressure at the correct pounds per square inch. Radial tires are better than

bias-ply tires. Also watch your inputs and speed and remember to adapt to the changing environment as you travel.

Off-Road Recovery

If something happens that causes you to leave the road surface while driving, there are several things that can be done to get you safely back onto the surface, regardless of the speed you are traveling. When the vehicle goes off the road, obviously the wheels will be turned to some degree. You need to keep this in mind because when you turn the wheel to an extreme angle, 25–35 degrees, the tire may stop rotating, depending on the type of surface you find yourself on and the speed at which you are traveling. This could be a bad thing.

When the tires stop rotating over the surface of the ground, they act like a board being pushed through the dirt. The weight, momentum, and forward speed of the vehicle push the tire over the ground. Loose gravel, sand, soft dirt, and landscaping rock build up on one side of the tire; when enough is built up, the tire will no longer be able to move forward through the surface. The tire will stop, but the vehicle won't. This is what causes vehicles to overturn when they go off-road.

When one side of the vehicle leaves the roadway, you need to avoid braking suddenly and immediately jerking the wheel to get back onto the surface. Instead, straighten the wheels to keep them rolling over the off-road surface, stay off all pedals, and allow the vehicle to slow down. As this occurs, gradually steer your vehicle back onto the road at a shallow angle. You need to hold the steering wheel steady through the whole process. Remember, *smooth* inputs.

Suppose you have no choice and are going to leave the road surface for whatever reason—e.g., going too fast through a curve, being forced off the road. You need to steer your vehicle off the road, rather than let it take you off. The greater control you have over your direction of travel, the better you can steer around obstacles and avoid damage to the vehicle. When braking, use as little of the brakes as possible, because you don't want to take away from your steering. The idea is to get the wheels straight, the speed down, and the vehicle gradually back on the road surface.

One more note about going off-road: if you are confident in your driving abilities and have tried the following maneuver at least once, when being pursued you can drop two of your tires off the side of the road surface in an area that has loose rock or gravel on the side. This will throw gravel at the vehicles behind you, possibly breaking their windshields and otherwise causing a distraction that will make them back off while you maintain control. Conversely, if you are pursuing someone, be aware of this possibility and don't let it happen to you.

Tire-Blowout Recovery

A blowout occurs with a sudden loss of air from a tire either in the front or rear wheel. To counteract this, you need to get off the brake but not let off the gas immediately. You might need to increase gas to counteract the new forces acting on the vehicle. The hardest thing is *not to brake*, but you mustn't. Continue to steer the vehicle and control the throttle. You need to bring the vehicle to a controlled stop, allowing it to slow down on its own enough so you can eventually brake safely and stop the vehicle in a controlled manner.

CHAPTER 11

Vehicle Dynamics

Vehicle dynamics is nothing more than the physical forces acting on the vehicle while it is in motion. When you drive a vehicle, you can only do two things: change speed and change direction. And there are physical forces at work on the vehicle that affect your ability to do these. If your input into the vehicle's controls exceeds these physical forces, then you lose control of the vehicle. That is why it is important for all drivers to understand the physical forces that affect the vehicle's ability to react to their actions. These factors include friction created between the tires and the road, momentum and inertia built up in the vehicle while in motion, and the centrifugal forces placed on the vehicle when its path is altered while in motion.

You must understand your vehicle's capabilities and what takes place as you operate the controls. As noted above, there are only two ways you can control a vehicle: changing speeds and changing directions. By using these two actions, you can cause the vehicle to perform three functions: it can go (changing speeds), it can stop (changing speeds), and it can turn (changing directions). You trigger these functions in one of four ways: by traveling forward or to the rear at a steady speed, by braking, by accel-

erating, or by turning. The most important thing to understand about vehicle dynamics is that for a vehicle to perform these four things there must be friction between the tires and the roadway, either stationary friction or rolling friction.

Several forces work on a vehicle during handling, and a small change in these can make a very big difference in the way a vehicle handles. Let's take a closer look at three primary forces we deal with when driving: friction, centrifugal and centripetal force, and weight shift.

FRICTION

All ground transportation vehicles are supported on the cushion of air in the four flexible rubber tires mounted on its wheels. If we had the ability to observe this from below a vehicle at rest, we would see four small patches of rubber, about 4 x 4 inches, resting on the road. These patches of rubber, known as "contact patches," are the only parts of the vehicle that physically touch the road surface. They create the necessary friction for your vehicle to go, stop, and turn. They are also your primary sources of the control feedback from the vehicle. It is important to know what makes the tires develop traction; it is even more important to know and understand what causes vehicles to lose that traction and become uncontrollable.

To review what we discussed in Chapter 10, static friction occurs when the vehicle is at rest, and 100 percent of friction is being used. Rolling friction is basically friction due to the motion of the tires; a tire rolling with good traction will have about 60 percent of its friction capability being used. Sliding friction results when the vehicle is in motion but the tires have no traction; this happens when the tires are sliding, locked, or skidding.

To have the ability to control the vehicle, you must maintain rolling friction between the tires and the road. When tires lose traction and start spinning or sliding, you can lose control of the vehicle. Two of these contact patches are the two in the front of the vehicle, which are used to steer. When your tires stop rolling, you lose the ability to steer. You already know that the steering wheel does not steer or turn the vehicle; it merely aims the front wheels in the desired direction. You also know that rolling friction is better than sliding friction, since once the tires have stopped rolling and started sliding, it is impossible to steer the vehicle in a controlled manner.

Every vehicle out there is just a machine, and there is a limit to what it can do at one time. You need to remember that every driver manipulation goes to the wheels, which in turn goes through the tires to those four contact patches. If 100 percent of that patch is braking, it cannot be turning. So to regain the ability to turn, you have to go from 100 percent to 40 percent brakes; then you have 60 percent of your steering ability.

Sometimes drivers try as hard as they can to force a vehicle past those limits. The maximum control capacity of the tire patches referred to earlier is called the "limit of adhesion." This is the limit of maximum performance available from a particular vehicle and tire design. If you force a vehicle to go beyond the limit of adhesion, then you lose traction and rolling friction. The vehicle is then out of control.

CENTRIFUGAL AND CENTRIPETAL FORCE

Centrifugal and centripetal force acting together allow you to drive around corners. When both forces are equal, you control the direction; if they are out of balance, you lose control.

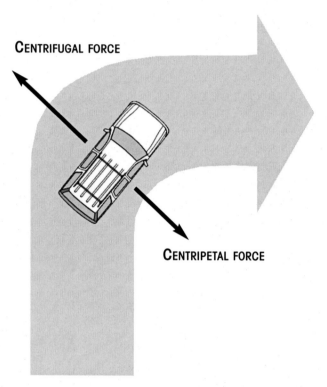

CENTRIFUGAL FORCE

CENTRIPETAL FORCE

When centrifugal and centripetal forces are equal, the vehicle travels in the desired direction.

WEIGHT SHIFT

Weight shift is a reaction to a change in the direction and/or speed of a vehicle. The shift occurs around the vehicle's center of mass. When the weight shift is forward or rearward, it is a longitudinal weight shift. When it is left or right, it is a lateral weight shift.

Weight transfer problems develop when the operator does too much steering and braking or too much accelerating and steering, which results in excessive weight transfer to the tires. When there is too much weight on the contact patches, the driver can lose control. When the steering wheel is turned, force pushes on the vehicle's center of gravity. If that force is greater than the vehicle can accept, it is possible for the vehicle to go out of control. The following factors determine the limit of adhesion: the vertical force placed on the tire; tire design; condition and type of road surface; amount of turning force; and, most important, speed of the vehicle.

With a little training and practice, you can feel when you are reaching the control limits of your vehicle long before those limits are exceeded and you lose control. Being able to feel the limits gives you more control and a better idea of what is taking place with the vehicle. Vehicles communicate to their drivers in two ways: how they ride (the vertical motion of the wheels and tires as they rise and fall over irregularities in the road surface) and how they handle (the vehicle's ability to remain in control when cornering or being driven through evasive maneuvers).

To understand the dynamics of a vehicle is to understand how G-forces affect the vehicle's handling anytime the steering wheel is moved while the vehicle is in motion. A lateral or sideways force is created (a force that pushes in the opposite direction from the direction the vehicle is turning). This force is an expression of inertia, or as stated in Newton's first law of motion (known as the law of inertia): "If a body is at rest or moving at a constant speed in a straight line it will remain at rest or keep moving in a straight line at constant speed unless it is acted upon by a force." One such force would be turning a steering wheel.

The vehicle has devices to help it deal with these outside forces and give the operator better control. An anti-sway bar is a spring steel bar mounted underneath a car at the front and rear. As the vehicle leans to once side, the bar is twisted. This in turn keeps the car level—by keeping the car from leaning with the weight shift in a turn, especially at high speed—and it keeps the center of gravity over the wheels, making it easier to control.

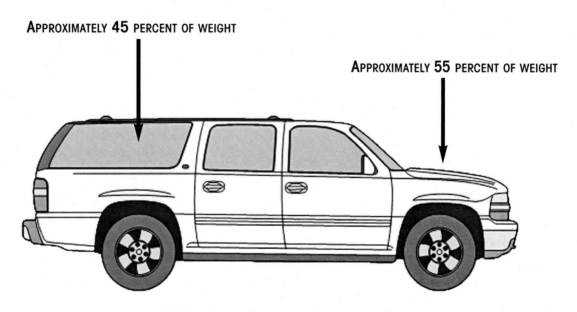

APPROXIMATELY **45** PERCENT OF WEIGHT

APPROXIMATELY **55** PERCENT OF WEIGHT

Weight distribution in a motionless vehicle.

LONGITUDINAL WEIGHT SHIFT

Weight is transferred to the front wheels, and rear wheels are lightened.

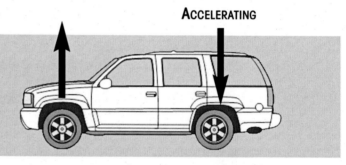

Weight is transferred to the rear wheels, and the front wheels are lightened.

LATERAL WEIGHT SHIFT

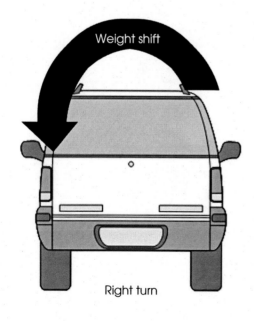

Right turn

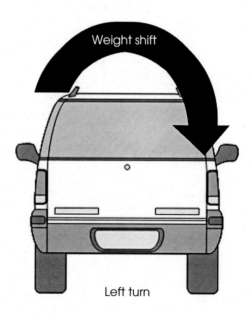

Left turn

CHAPTER 12

Vehicle Evasion Maneuvers

You have done all the right things—heightened your awareness, increased visible security measures, analyzed all the routes used, performed surveillance detection—and the attack is occurring anyway. So what do you do now? What *can* you do? These two questions are best answered by what is happening when you recognize that the attack is taking place. The closer you are, the more limited your options. Two options you do have are the forward 180-degree turn and the reverse 180-degree turn.

FORWARD 180-DEGREE TURN

The forward 180-degree turn, or "bootleg turn," is used when you recognize the attack from a distance and have enough speed to perform it. Its only restrictions are enough area and enough speed to complete it.

You notice a barricade or an attack taking shape to the front, and you are still four to five car lengths away. You do not want to go into the attack area or kill zone. There are several ways to avoid this. If you are traveling at least 35–40 mph on a dry, hard surface and have unrestricted movement to the side for your vehicle, you can perform a forward 180-degree turn.

When you see the threat, lock your parking brake. This engages the rear braking system of the vehicle, and the rear wheels will start sliding at that speed. Once the rear wheels are sliding, turn the steering wheel one-quarter turn toward the open road area or the area with the fewest obstructions. *Do not turn the wheel more than one-quarter of a turn.* Turning the wheel one-quarter turn will cause your vehicle to rotate about 180 degrees. When it has completed its rotation, you should be facing the opposite direction. You can now release the parking brake and speed away from the attack site.

On wet surfaces, you should be traveling at a slower rate of speed because your vehicle will slide more quickly and you don't want to overrotate and end up doing a 360-degree turn. If you feel you are starting to overrotate, you can use the normal brake of the car and control the speed of rotation. Once you are facing away from the attack area, release the parking brake and move out.

This sounds like a lot to remember, and in a high-stress situation it is. So try to remember this mnemonic: "Don't turn the wheel until you hear the squeal." This will help you remember not to turn your steering wheel until you hear the squeal of the rear wheels locking up and sliding. The best way to get proficient at this or any other technique is through practice.

REVERSE 180-DEGREE TURN

The reverse 180-degree turn, or "J" turn, can be used in a variety of ways if you don't have the speed to do a forward 180 but are still not in the attack area, or if someone is attempting an overrun attack on your vehicle while it is moving. The restriction for the reverse 180 is that you cannot have any traffic to the rear of your vehicle. But it is important to remember one thing in vehicle evasion: people tend to believe that speed is the best way to go, and when something happens they floor it and never let up. Speed should be used only to gain distance between you and the threat or to get someone to a medical facility if his condition is critical. It is not advisable to run at 100 mph at all times, especially when escaping the threat. At that speed you will be dodging other vehicles and people, and you will probably miss turns and eventually have an accident.

In this next scenario, you are closer to the attack zone than before, or you have movement restrictions to the front or sides so you cannot do the forward 180 and you have unrestricted movement to the rear. Your best option is the reverse 180.

As soon as you notice the threat, stop the vehicle completely. While you are stopping, shift the vehicle into reverse and then floor the gas pedal and accelerate backward in as straight as line as possible. As you go, count up to 4 seconds, which means you are traveling about 20 to 25 mph and you have enough momentum to perform the maneuver. Once you hit the 4-second count, take your foot off the accelerator and turn the wheel as quickly as possible toward the open road or an unobstructed area, locking the steering wheel at its limit. The violent and quick spinning of the front wheels will cause the front tires to lose their grip on the surface, causing the front of the vehicle to slide around, pivoting on the rear tires. As the vehicle is moving around in its arc, begin to rotate the steering wheel in a countersteer back to its original start; you should now be facing 180 degrees away from the attack. Quickly put your car

into drive and move away from the threat as quickly as possible.

Two things to remember with the 180 reverse turn: do not use your brakes, and do not have your foot on the gas as you are shifting the car back into drive, because this could damage your transmission and decrease your chances of escaping the threat.

VEHICLE BARRICADE BREACHING

Vehicle barricade breaching, often referred to as ramming, is much simpler than it sounds.

Not only is your vehicle your best means of escaping a threat, but it is also the best weapon when your options are limited. If you do not notice the attack until you are in your attackers' zone of control and your movement to the rear is restricted or obstructed, then your options are limited. As soon as you notice the barricade or an attack forming to the front, the driver and every person in your vehicle need to start looking to the sides. Most initial fire will come from there and will be directed at the driver. If your attackers can kill the driver, then they have effectively stopped the vehicle and limited your response. If you are two to three car lengths away from the barricade, you need to stop and maintain that distance. This will cause the attackers to move into the open, forcing them to discard the cover or disguise they were using to blend in. Since you have not entered into their planned area of control, they will now have to come to you.

When your vehicle is stopped, rotate your hands to the bottom of the steering wheel. This allows you to maintain control of the wheel if the air bag deploys. Do not worry about the air bag; it will deflate fast enough that it will not limit your vision. You then sight in on the area of the vehicle you intend to ram. Your ideal hit is the rear wheel, because this area has the least amount of weight for you to push out of the way. When lining up the vehicle, you want to strike the strongest part of your vehicle against the strongest part of the attackers' vehicle, so you are aiming the long frame of your vehicle against their axle.

You then floor the gas. At two to three car lengths' distance from the vehicle, you will get to about 15–25 mph, about the speed at which you want to strike the vehicle. It is enough to rotate the blocking vehicle out of the way, and at this speed it will cause minimal damage to your vehicle, which is important because you want to get as far away as possible from the attack site, as quickly as possible. The more speed with which you hit that stationary vehicle, the more damage will happen to yours. You line up your driver's-side headlight on the rear wheel of the blocking vehicle and then shift your car into low gear and accelerate. As you strike the vehicle, keep your hand on the gearshift and your foot on the accelerator to speed through the barricade and keep your wheel straight. If you lock fenders with the barricade vehicle, keep your foot on the gas and jiggle the wheel back and forth until the two cars are unlocked, and accelerate away. Don't forget to shift your gear back into drive.

Ramming is so easy because, as explained earlier, any vehicle is only connected to the earth by four pieces of rubber. You are breaking the contact of two of those pieces and moving only about one-third of the vehicle's weight. Where you hit the barricading vehicle is very important; the closer you strike to the center of the car, the more weight you are trying to shift. If you hit the exact center, or T, of the vehicle, you are pushing 100 percent of its weight with 100 percent of your vehicle's weight. If you hit the vehicle correctly over one of its axles, then you are pushing around one-third of its weight with 100 percent of yours.

The following are some points to remember about vehicle ramming.

- You should know whether your vehicle has an automatic fuel cut-off; this is a device that shuts of the flow of fuel from the gas tank to the engine in an accident. If your vehicle has one, you need to know how to reset it, because you don't want to bypass the barricade and then run out of gas 50 feet away.
- You might not always be able to strike the vehicle in the rear. You can strike the front of the vehicle; it will just be a little bit more impact.
- When the target vehicle is pulling out in front of you as you are moving, never strike it in the area of its direction of travel. You need to strike it in the area from which it came; otherwise its momentum will carry it into your car as you pass.
- You need to keep your hand on the gearshift. In some cars, the impact can cause a vehicle to jump out of gear.
- Do not worry about the damage to your vehicle. A car can travel a long way with a busted radiator, an oil leak, or a flat tire, and your immediate need is to get as far away as quickly as you can to a safe area.

This technique will not work on commercial vehicles, such as bulldozers or dump trucks, where there is an extreme weight difference. Also, if your wheelbase is a lot higher than the height of the barricading vehicle, you need to make sure that you don't drive over the top and flip your vehicle or go airborne.

If you remember nothing else, remember to move! You can go either forward or back, but get out of the attackers' area of control. Stay alive!

If you see the attack shaping up in front, it is inadvisable to take side roads if you have not done a route analysis of those roads. You have no idea whether they dead-end or are even passable. The best bet is always to go back the way you just came; you did not notice any threats when you came through, and it is probably your closest safe haven. If you cannot retrace your route, then go forward through the attack zone along your preplanned route. This keeps you on a familiar road with known safe havens.

Never try to drive around a barricade. For one thing, you don't know what you might have to drive over, and you want to disrupt the barricade as much as possible to distract the attackers. Any damage you do to their vehicle will reduce the chances of their pursuing you. If you are trapped in a moving barricade, remember the vehicle-barricade-breaching principles: attack one of the side vehicles at its axle, pushing through and escaping; if stopped at a traffic control point and you can attack the axle of a side vehicle to get out, do it—it will still work. Remember, you are breaking the traction of two 4 x 4 pieces of rubber. *Move and live.*

You need to know a few other things when moving out of the attack zone and trying to get to a known safe area. When driving over curbs, you need to attack them at an angle of 30 to 40 degrees at 30 mph. Never strike the curb head-on; you might blow your tire. If you strike it at less than 30 degrees, you might knock the tire off the rim. Be prepared for a big bump. Don't worry about driving on a sidewalk, breaking the law, running over outdoor furniture, or making people get out of your way. Remember, you are trying to stay alive. If you honk the horn, people will move out of the way, and furniture is replaceable.

The hardest part about ramming is overcoming a lifetime of training to avoid accidents. You must strike the barricading vehicle. Your attackers are not going to make an insurance claim against you. Hit the vehicle—not only does it move the barricade out of the way, but by disturbing the vehicle your attackers, who were using it as a shield, now

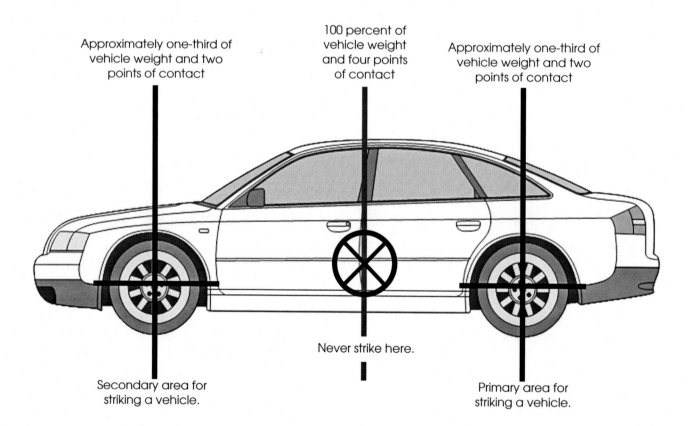

Approximately one-third of vehicle weight and two points of contact

100 percent of vehicle weight and four points of contact

Approximately one-third of vehicle weight and two points of contact

Never strike here.

Secondary area for striking a vehicle.

Primary area for striking a vehicle.

have to think about getting out of its way instead of shooting at you as you drive by. Surprise works both ways; by surprising the attackers with these tactics, you are slowing their reaction time and forcing them to think and react to you.

If you encounter a barricade and have neither the time nor the distance to come to a complete stop, slow down as if you are going to stop. Hopefully, this will force your attackers to react. You then drop the gear into low and ram the barricade, using the same principles outlined above. Just be careful of your speed. Drivers who do a moving ram instead of coming to a complete stop

sometimes let adrenaline take over and strike the barricade at too high a rate of speed, causing excessive damage to their vehicle when there is no need.

When passing the vehicle or the barricade, you should expect to take fire. Whenever someone is shooting at your vehicle, you need to place yourself and the passengers below the window line of the vehicle. If a round penetrates the car body, it might be slowed down sufficiently to do less damage to a body.

Do you always have to ram forward? No, you can also ram to the rear to get yourself out of that danger area.

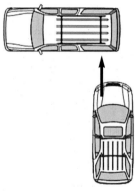

1. Line up the headlight on the axle.

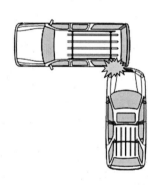

2. Accelerate, striking the target point.

3. Make contact, keeping your foot on the accelerator.

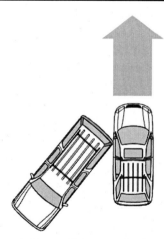

4. You push the vehicle out of the way as you accelerate and make your escape.

RAMMING FORWARD TO CLEAR A DANGER AREA

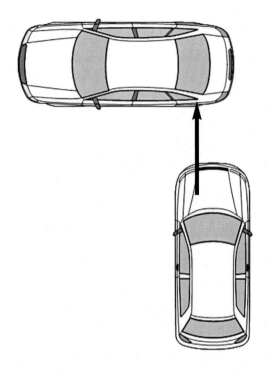

Aiming point when striking the rear of the barricading vehicle.

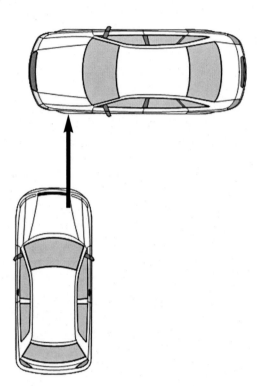

Aiming point when striking the front of the barricading vehicle.

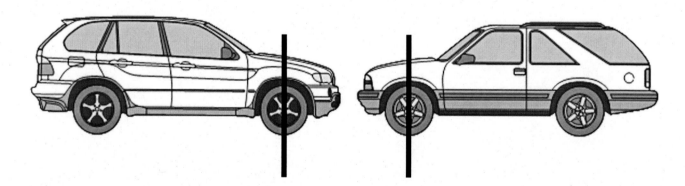

When confronted by a two-car barricade, you cannot ram both, so pick one as your target and forget about the other. Moving one vehicle will allow you enough room to escape the attack. The following two drawings show how two-vehicle barricades can be set up differently and the striking points for each.

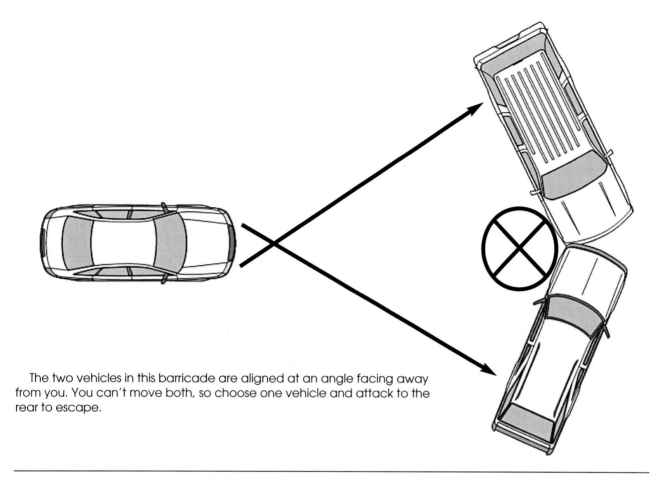

The two vehicles in this barricade are aligned at an angle facing away from you. You can't move both, so choose one vehicle and attack to the rear to escape.

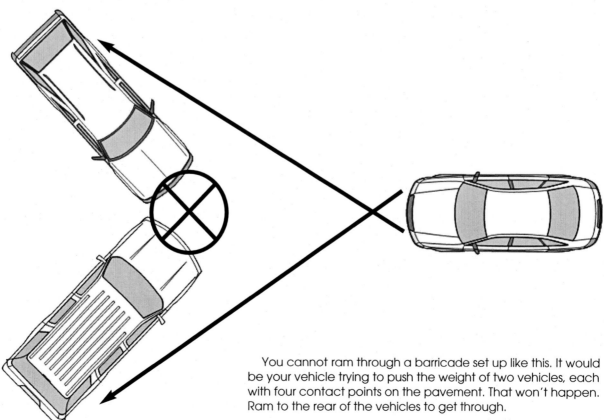

You cannot ram through a barricade set up like this. It would be your vehicle trying to push the weight of two vehicles, each with four contact points on the pavement. That won't happen. Ram to the rear of the vehicles to get through.

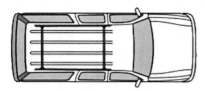

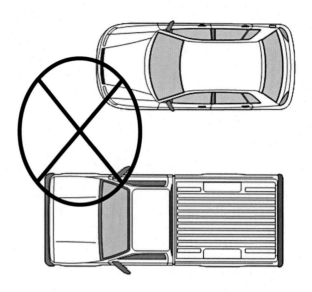

You cannot ram through a vehicle head-on. Instead drive around and move to the nearest safe area.

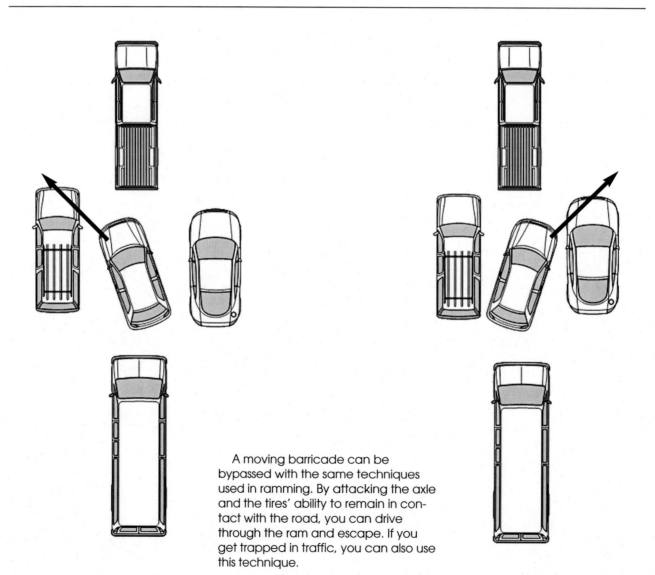

A moving barricade can be bypassed with the same techniques used in ramming. By attacking the axle and the tires' ability to remain in contact with the road, you can drive through the ram and escape. If you get trapped in traffic, you can also use this technique.

RAMMING REARWARD TO CLEAR A DANGER AREA

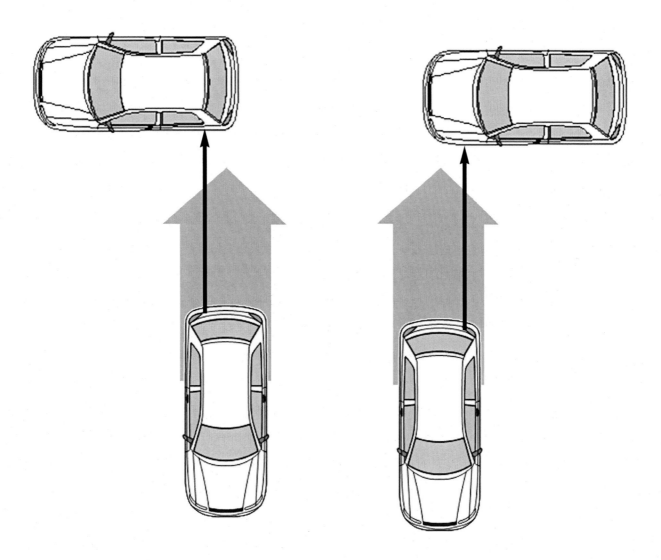

Aiming point when striking the rear of
the barricading vehicle.

Aiming point when striking the front of
the barricading vehicle.

CHAPTER 13

Attack Scenarios

Historically, most vehicle attacks have taken place in urban environments, and when committed against a moving vehicle they have generally been one of two types: the overrun or the stationary roadblock attack. However, you should keep in mind that the type of attack is limited only by the imagination of the perpetrator and that, through his actions, the victim himself often dictates not only the time and location of the attack but also ultimately the type of attack used (see Chapter 16, "Case Studies of Actual Vehicle Attacks").

OVERRUN ATTACK

The overrun attack (known as a *drive-by* in the United States) is the most common type of vehicle attack and usually happens when the attackers don't know your routes or patterns. Overruns are very easy to carry out and are used extensively all over the world with great success. The threat selects the victim because of his discernible routine, which makes him time and place predictable. The victim himself actually determines the attack site and method of attack through his lack of security awareness and his failure to vary his routines and routes. The attackers will then choose the best site for the attack to take place, and through surveillance they will learn the capa-

bilities of the victim's car, driver, and, of course, the victim himself. The attackers can use either a single vehicle or multiple vehicles carrying three to four men in each.

When ready to attack the target, the ambushers will wait somewhere along the victim's route or follow the victim's car from a known location. The area they preselect to start their attack will have some type of movement-control measures in place, and it will be a spot where the target cannot take evasive action. As the target is distracted or when they think the victim is not paying attention, the attackers will pull out to pass, fire at the victim as they pass, and continue to drive away, making their escape along a preplanned route.

The best way to protect yourself while driving is to not allow anyone to pass or pull alongside your vehicles, and to not pass any vehicle until it has pulled to the side and the driver has gotten out.

Vehicle-Borne IEDs

A type of overrun attack favored by terrorists in Iraq and elsewhere is the vehicle-borne IED (VBIED), usually directed at any target of opportunity. The attackers are looking for convoys of either military or civilian contractors, which are usually very easy to pick out because of the types of vehicles they drive.

The threat identifies the target vehicle, drives up on it to pass, and then detonates the explosive device. Or the attackers slow down as convoys come up to pass them and then move toward the convoy and detonate their vehicle. Sometimes the attackers drive slowly or stop at traffic circles, waiting for targets of opportunity, and then speed up or slow down as if attempting to merge into the convoy.

VBIEDs can also come from the opposite direction and either detonate as they pass or ram a vehicle and then detonate. Again, avoid being time and place predictable, as well as remaining aware of your surroundings and alert to threats. Remember, this type of attack is used for targets of opportunity, which is why it is important to have a vehicle that blends in so the enemy will not notice you and instead will go for the more visible targets.

Be alert for vehicles coming at you head-on. Determine whether the driver is being erratic or weaving as if he is thinking about crossing the line. If possible, avoid roads without a median separating the lanes of traffic. Any road without medians makes it easy for someone to cross over to ram or detonate against your motorcade.

Motorcycle or Scooter Attack

The last type of overrun attack we will examine is one using a motorcycle or scooter. In most countries, these vehicles can move through traffic without being noticed, especially at traffic control points and stop lights. It is common to see these vehicles drive between vehicles to get to the front of the traffic. So it is easy for the threat to follow the target's vehicle until it stops, and then drive up on the victim, open fire, and escape. This type of attack happens so much in some European countries that they have passed laws making it illegal for these motorcycles or scooters to carry passengers. This does not mean that the driver cannot fire at you, however. Be aware of these types of vehicles, especially when you are stopped or moving in traffic.

You should also be aware of bicycles, which have been used several times in the

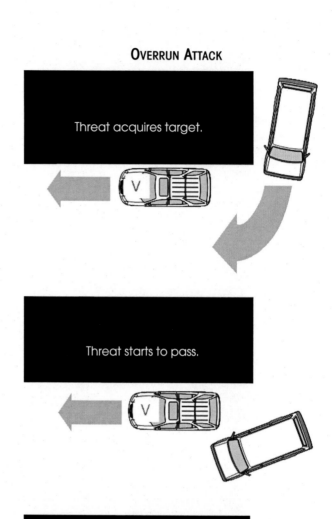

OVERRUN ATTACK

Threat acquires target.

Threat starts to pass.

Threat opens fire.

After firing, the threat drives away on his escape route.

Remember to drive in the left or outer lane of traffic. This prevents the threat from being able to drive alongside your vehicle and shoot your driver. Plus, there are fewer areas to shoot from on this side of the vehicle.

VEHICLE-BORNE IED ATTACK

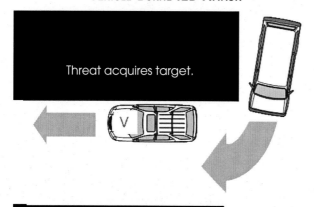

Threat acquires target.

Threat pulls up alongside victim.

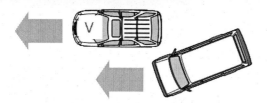

Be suspicious of vehicles that wait until you pass to pull out into traffic or that weave through traffic to get next to you.

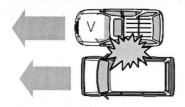

Threat detonates VBIED.

There is no need for the attackers to plan an escape, so this eliminates an element of planning.

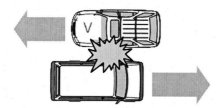

The VBIED could come at you head-on and detonate after he rams you or while coming alongside.

STATIONARY VEHICLE IED ATTACK

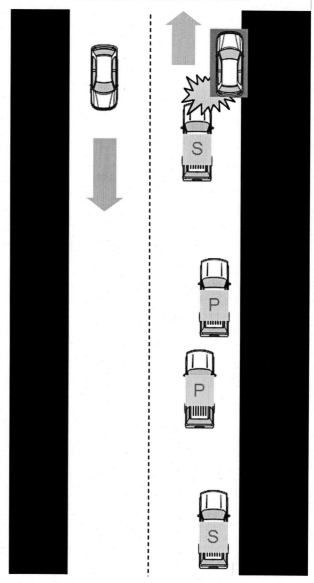

If a vehicle is blocking your route, it is not your responsibility to move it! If no driver is present or locals are not attempting to move it, you must consider it a VBIED. You can either drive around the danger, staying as far away as possible; take an alternate route; or return to your safe area. In Iraq there have been several instances where abandoned vehicles armed with VBIEDs have been command-detonated when someone tried to move them from blocking the road. The military or police authority has the responsibility for moving these obstructions from the road. Drive your routes regularly to ensure that they are clear. This caution also holds true for vehicles that are on the side of the road with no one present. Do not drive right next to them; maintain a safe distance as you pass.

ROADSIDE IED ATTACKS

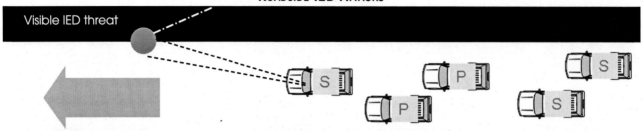

Visible IED threat

IED attacks are sometimes initiated with a visible device and a wire leading off the road. A vigilant security detail will see this evidence, stop, and call for help. The bad guys know this, so they position the fake decoys where they can be seen and set up the real IEDs where they think the vehicles will stop. Once the vehicles are stopped and people are moving around, then they detonate the real device.

Never stop your car or the convoy in response to a visible threat. Once you stop, you are a sitting target. If you are not going to drive by the suspected device, back up or turn around and leave the area, or cross the road. Be careful driving over medians even if you see locals doing it. Most explosive devices are command-detonated, and the person watching can usually tell the difference between locals and nonlocals.

MOTORCYCLE OR SCOOTER ATTACKS

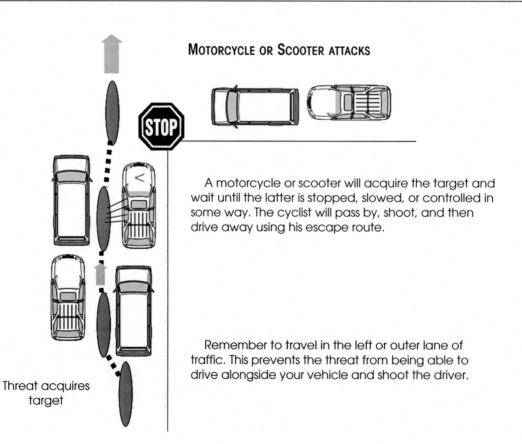

A motorcycle or scooter will acquire the target and wait until the latter is stopped, slowed, or controlled in some way. The cyclist will pass by, shoot, and then drive away using his escape route.

Remember to travel in the left or outer lane of traffic. This prevents the threat from being able to drive alongside your vehicle and shoot the driver.

Threat acquires target

A vehicle headed against traffic is called a *kamikaze*, which is something personal security detachments watch out for as possible VBIEDs. The people sitting around the curb in the traffic circle with packages also need to be watched. Traffic circles are natural choke points, since you have to slow down when entering them, making you an easier target.

When this kamikaze on the right was checked out, it had women and children in it and therefore was not considered a threat. Most VBIEDs have a single occupant, but you should never assume that women and children are harmless.

Middle East to carry IEDs. Be alert for any bicycle that carries a larger than normal load, has a battery visible, or exhibits any other suspicious appearance.

STATIONARY ROADBLOCK ATTACK

A stationary roadblock attack is not used as often as an overrun attack, because it requires the attackers to know the intended target's routes and patterns. The attackers will park their vehicles around corners or on the downside of a hill, somewhere the approaching victim cannot observe them. By the time the attackers' vehicles are observed, the target has no opportunity to turn around or avoid the roadblock. The attackers will then move forward and either kill the target if their goal is assassination or force the target out of his vehicle and drive away if their goal is kidnapping.

CONSIDERATIONS WHILE MOVING

Drive in the far left lane whenever possible so that your vehicle cannot be forced to the curb or against a vehicle parked on the side of the road. When you are stopped in traffic, remember to stay in the lane that will allow the best maneuverability out of any crisis. Route analysis will tell you which one this is. You always need to allow at least 8 to 10 feet between your vehicle and the one in front of you when you are stopped, and you need to think about this all the time. Some people have the habit of pulling up as close

Perfectly normal traffic control point with little or no traffic with an overpass. If you stay in the center lane, though, there is a chance of getting trapped. Outside lanes are best.

Unless you are the first vehicle at the light at an underpass, you will get blocked in. If you are not in the right lane, you will not be able to drive on the shoulder. A good route analysis will help you plan for these situations.

as possible to the car in front of them. If you do this, you will not have the room to maneuver your vehicle into another lane if you need to. One way to gauge if you are far enough from the vehicle in front of you is to look over the hood of your car at the ground in front of you; if your hood is about 1 foot behind the rear tire of the vehicle in front of you, you are far enough apart that you won't lock bumpers when you try to turn.

While driving in your vehicle, you will run into many day-to-day situations that could force you to stop or alter your course. The following are some of the more common situations you may encounter.

Traffic Accidents

Traffic accidents are very common all over they world. Depending on how bad it is, the number of vehicles involved, and the number and extent of the casualties, an accident can ensnarl traffic for miles. And as you know, being stopped in traffic makes you vulnerable to attack. Terrorist groups and criminals know this as well and have faked accidents (and will continue to fake them) because this tactic works. By exploiting the "Good Samaritan" nature of most people, they can lure unsuspecting targets into a trap.

When an accident happens on a stretch of road that you are traveling on—whether you are involved in the accident or not—you need to assess the situation seriously to determine whether it is a ruse to get your vehicle or convoy stopped.

If You Are Involved in the Accident

If you are involved in a minor accident and you have the ability to move your vehicle, do so and then pull up about a block away. While you are driving away, keep an eye on the surrounding area, and then pull over. This forces the attackers to react to your driving off. Since you have moved out of their preplanned attack zone, they will need to stop you any way they can, so they will probably draw weapons. If you observe any type of hostile action or pursuit once you

pull over to observe, you need to leave the area immediately and head toward your closest safe haven.

If you feel the accident is a ruse, leave the scene immediately and drive to your work, the U.S. Embassy, or other safe area. Tell embassy staff or security people what happened and why you felt threatened enough to leave. Ask them to report the accident and your involvement to the local police as soon as possible. It's better to drive away when you feel uncomfortable with a situation and deal with the local police later than to become a victim.

If You Are Not Involved in the Accident

When you come upon an accident or other roadside emergency, you need to scrutinize the scene carefully. Did you see the accident take place? If you actually saw it and the cars are banged up, then the accident is probably real, since something like that is hard to stage and time. Look over the accident, judge how bad it is, call it in, and leave the area. You are not a trained medic, and you are not there to provide assistance, so there is no reason to stop.

Some factors to consider when determining if an accident is real or staged include the following:

- Are the victims of the accident trying to wave down everyone or just you? If they are allowing other vehicles to pass without trying to flag them down, but start waving their arms or signaling in some other way at you to stop, then the accident is probably not real, since anyone in a real accident would want help from whoever could provide it.
- Is a crowd gathering at the accident site? Most accidents will draw a crowd, and traffic will slow way down because people want to gawk at the wreck and try to help. So if there is no crowd or traffic jam, then something is wrong.
- Where is the accident located? Is it an isolated area with little or no lighting or traffic (i.e., a good place for an ambush)?

A car wreck is one way to stop or slow traffic. If your vehicles are not involved in the accident, keep moving.

In some countries, the law requires that the first person at the scene of an accident stop and render assistance. But if you are the first person to arrive at an accident scene, you need to look at your environment and think about the things we just talked about. If you feel uncomfortable, use your cell phone or radio to call in the accident and keep going. It is better to get a ticket than become a victim.

Checkpoints

Whether you are overseas or in the States, you always face the possibility of being stopped by police or military (or paramilitary in some countries) officials, either individually or at a checkpoint.

First off, you need to remember your threat assessment and working environment. When you did your research into the tactics used by the terrorist or criminal elements in your area, did they include impersonating the police or military? As you approach the situation, you need to be very cautious, heighten your awareness level, and start looking for the unusual from as far away as possible. The farther away you can identify the threat, the farther you are from the planned kill zone.

You need to look at the people and vehicles at the checkpoint; a legitimate law enforcement or military organization will have a uniform standard to follow. Of course, this means you need to know what type of uniforms and equipment the police and the military use in the area so that you can spot any discrepancies. Pay particular attention to the footwear—it's easy to steal a uniform; it's harder to get a pair of regulation shoes or boots that fit.

Observe the weapons carefully as well. Once again, a legitimate military or law enforcement unit will have uniform weapons and standards about how they are carried and maintained. Know what the standards and weapons are for your areas of operation.

Look at their vehicles as well. The vehicles in police and military units should be alike—colors, lights, how they are marked, and where. This is another area you need to research so that you can recognize fakes if they appear.

You also need to be aware of radios. Most legitimate law enforcement personnel will have some type of radio communication with higher headquarters, so look for the officer who pulled you over to be talking on the radio. If this doesn't happen, be suspicious.

If the weapons, clothing, belts, badges, caps, footwear, and equipment are uniform, that is a good sign that the personnel are probably legitimate. But every piece of police or military equipment, gear, or clothing discussed can be made or stolen, and you should also consider that the police or military personnel can be helping the terrorists or criminals.

Now you need to consider the location and makeup of the stop. Legitimate checkpoints or roadblocks, regardless of country, will have some factors in common. They are usually located on straight stretches of a road or highway so that law enforcement personnel can observe approaching vehicles and take action if any vehicles turn around. This also gives tractor-trailer trucks more room to come to a stop because of their size and momentum. Legitimate checkpoints are usually marked so people know what to expect, as well as having lights for safety reasons (especially at night), cones to divide the road into lanes for faster service, and a designated holding area for people and vehicles that need more scrutiny. Official vehicles should be present at the checkpoint or barricade. If there are no official vehicles—only civilian vehicles or no vehicles at all—be ready to take evasive action.

The conduct of the people manning the checkpoint or roadblock is also important. Are they waving all vehicles in front of you through without checking? As you approach, do they place their hands on their weapons or point out your vehicle to others? Are they using their weapons and acting in an intimidating manner? Observing any abnormal behavior can help you determine if the checkpoint is legitimate.

If police or military officers do halt you, remain in your vehicle and keep your engine running if possible. When an officer asks to speak to you or for your documents, lower the window just enough to be able to speak or pass the documents through. (Of course, you should have made sure that all the papers you need for travel are ready, available, and correct before you departed. These papers include vehicle registration, driver's license, travel permits if needed, and weapons permits if you or your security personnel are armed, because you want to be able to pass through these checkpoints without causing an incident or bringing any unnecessary attention to yourself.) Everyone in the vehicle should be polite but alert for any unusual actions by the officers or other individuals in the area. If the situation becomes unusual or turns bad, leave the area immediately and proceed to the nearest safe haven (e.g., the embassy or your office). Report the incident and explain why you took the actions you did.

Never allow yourself to become boxed in or separated from your vehicle or security. When approaching an unexpected roadblock, call your office or someone you trust and tell that person what is happening and your location so that, if anything does happen, there will be a starting point for the response.

Finally, know the unwritten rules for the area. In some countries, roadblocks are a way for police or military personnel to earn extra money. If this is accepted in the country you are in, make sure you have what is necessary to be allowed through without too much harassment. Do not be disrespectful to checkpoint staff. If they hint that you should pay and you know it is done there, pay up and avoid trouble.

If you are traveling in a security convoy, the drivers should pull all the vehicles to the roadblock a little offset so that they can see what is taking place and can back up without hitting each other if they need to. The security lead should collect all the information for your vehicles and present it all at once. If the crew at the roadblock ask everyone to get out of the vehicles, all security personnel should get out with weapons at the ready and their doors partially opened. The driver and nonsecurity personnel should remain in the vehicles.

Foreign roadblocks and checkpoints can be very tense, high-risk situations, depending on the threat level in the day-to-day environment of that country. You should know the

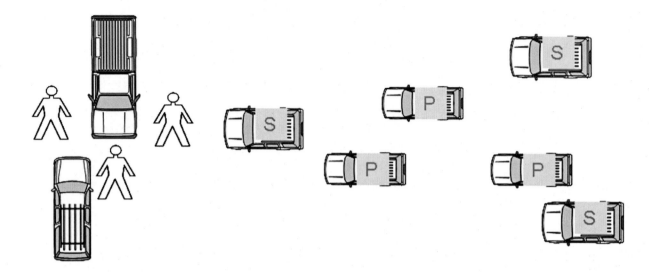

When approaching a roadblock, the lead security vehicle pulls forward to investigate. The passenger vehicles pull up behind but slightly offset so that everyone has a greater field of view. The two rear security vehicles pull off to the side behind the passenger vehicles to observe down both sides and to the rear. If there is a problem, this alignment will allow the passenger vehicles to back away without having to wait for other vehicles to get out of the way. The security vehicles closest to the threat will move and begin providing cover fire. The lead vehicle will remain to help with the threat, and the vehicles not engaged will escort the passenger vehicles away from the threat. When the passenger vehicles are clear, the two security vehicles will disengage and move after the detail.

customs of the country, be flexible, and do what is needed to get yourself rolling again.

Forced Immobilization Tactics

We have all seen television shows or movies in which the bad guys crash into the good guys' vehicle, trying to force it off the road. In real life, this technique won't work unless there is a major difference in the weights of the vehicles. Just as we discussed in the earlier section on ramming, if you have equal weights exerting equal force on each other, then a stalemate results and the only effect is psychological. When a car strikes you in the middle, it cannot force you off the road. Concentrate on driving your vehicle to a safe area. Don't let these tactics distract you from driving and paying attention to your surroundings.

Remember, speed is not your friend in a car fight. Keep your speed under 35 mph. The faster you go, the less rubber your tires put on the pavement and the easier it is to make you lose control of your vehicle and

stop you. Sudden braking and accelerating or sharp turns away will confuse your attacker and stress him out, leading to errors on his part. Let him make the mistakes so you can get away.

Always try to keep the pursuing vehicle behind you. As it swings from side to side trying to pass you, hit your brakes briefly when it is behind you. This will make the driver brake or hit the rear of your vehicle, which does nothing more than push you ahead and could damage his engine or radiator.

PIT Technique

The precision immobilization technique, or PIT (sometimes called pursuit intervention technique), is used by law enforcement agencies in this country—and sometimes you see it accidentally happen in NASCAR. This tactic uses the same principles of ramming, i.e., attacking the vehicle where there is the least amount of weight and only two contact points. The only difference is that you do PIT while you are moving. The driver of the attacking

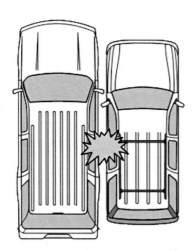

Two vehicles slamming into each other cancel each other out, since 100 percent of each vehicle's weight is working against the other.

You cannot be forced off this way either. Here you have less than half of the attacking vehicle's weight trying to push 100 percent of yours, and you have all four vehicle contact points on the ground.

vehicle will try to position his vehicle on either side at the rear corner panel or the body of your vehicle behind the rear wheel. Once the attacker gets into this position, he will turn his vehicle into yours, making contact. This causes your two rear contact points to lose their contact with the ground and slide. The attacker will then accelerate and drive through, whipping your vehicle around the front of his vehicle. There is no way to stop this technique if it is executed properly. At speeds of more than 40 mph, it can be dangerous, possibly causing the victim to flip.

Always protect your rear quarter panels so a pursuer cannot do this to you. Do this by braking suddenly and then accelerating, or by steering away from the attacking car when it makes contact and then accelerating a little. The latter will shift your vehicle's weight back to the point of contact, making it harder for the attacking vehicle to break your contact patches.

If the attacker is directly behind you or passing behind you to change sides, you should brake. This will cause him to brake as he passes behind you; if he is directly behind you, he will hit the rear of your vehicle. Once again, this cannot stop you, but it may damage his vehicle and take him out of the pursuit. Again, stay around 35 mph and do not let stress dictate your actions.

Another use for PIT is to move vehicles out of the way during movement either in a convoy or a single vehicle. Sometimes honking the horn is not enough, and people overseas especially tend to ignore this. During movement, you do not want to be traveling 5 mph or get boxed in by slow-moving vehicles. Your lead vehicle can use the technique to move those vehicles out of the way and continue on in a safe manner. Just remember, never use this technique when you are going faster than 35 mph because it can cause the vehicle you strike to roll. Also be careful when using this technique in crowded urban environments—you could cause a major accident. *But do what you need to do to stay safe.*

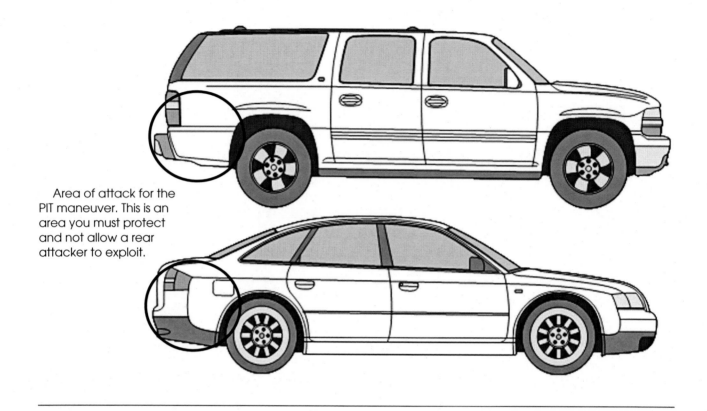

Area of attack for the PIT maneuver. This is an area you must protect and not allow a rear attacker to exploit.

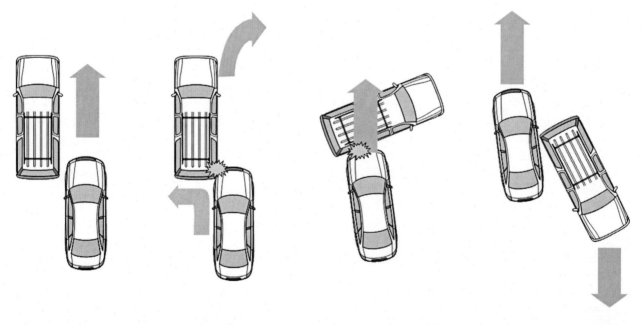

Attacker maneuvers into position at the rear quarter panel; it does not matter which side.

Contact is made, breaking the victim's rear traction and starting the slide as the attacker accelerates through.

The victim whips around the front of the attacking vehicle.

The victim's car is spun out and effectively stopped by the attacker.

CONSIDERATIONS WHILE STOPPED

Even though it is best to continue moving, you will probably not be able to stay in constant movement, especially in an urban environment. Eventually traffic, stoplights or stop signs, or some other impediment will stop you. As we discussed earlier in the section on moving considerations, your route analysis will tell you whether you want to travel in the inner lanes (to prevent your vehicle from being forced to the curb) or outer lanes (so you have the option of turning off if necessary and limiting overrun attacks). Avoid the center lanes at all times. This is also important when you are stopped: you don't want to have the vehicle trapped so that you are prevented from turning and running either left or right, onto a sidewalk, or into another lane of travel. Your route analysis will let you know what is available at each stop and which lanes you might get boxed in and which lanes provide you with the best options for escape.

Molotov Cocktail Attack

Several types of attacks can take place while you are stopped, including the use of a Molotov cocktail. This weapon is not much of a threat if you have a hardtop and keep the windows up and doors locked. However, if your windows are down and the container gets inside, then you will be in

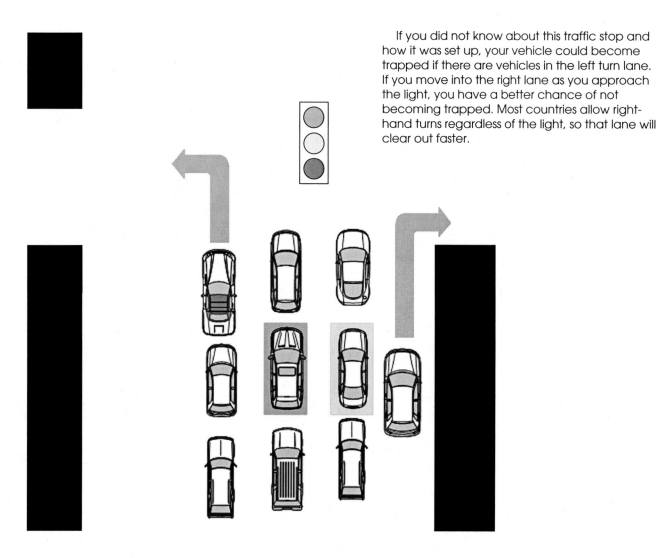

If you did not know about this traffic stop and how it was set up, your vehicle could become trapped if there are vehicles in the left turn lane. If you move into the right lane as you approach the light, you have a better chance of not becoming trapped. Most countries allow right-hand turns regardless of the light, so that lane will clear out faster.

trouble. Also, a softtop on a vehicle will burn, so don't choose one. Forget about what you see in the films; the initial flame will burn brightly for about 40 seconds and scorch your paint, nothing more. Remember to keep a fire extinguisher inside the vehicle.

When you are stopped, all the passengers in all your vehicles need to keep their eyes open for what is taking place around them. Be aware of men, women, and children carrying packages or bottles that might be thrown at your vehicle. If your vehicle is totally blocked or disabled, wait 8 to 10 seconds for the initial flames to subside before exiting. If possible, stay put in your vehicle where you are safer but continue to assess the situation.

Standoff Weapon Attack

Another type of attack on stopped vehicles is the standoff weapon attack done with rocket-propelled grenades (RPGs), sniper weapons, or other types of shoulder-fired weapons. To fire a shoulder-fired weapon

your attacker will need specific terrain: he has to have visibility to aim, the clearance so he can track the vehicle for a moving shot, a clear field of fire for a stationary shot, and an area for the back blast to go. During the stop, you, your security team and other passengers need to scan the rooftops, looking for the best firing positions for shoulder-fired weapons because of the back blast; any alleys or empty areas between buildings; and basically any place where there is a clear field of fire toward your vehicles.

In the Middle East and South America, several attacks on stopped vehicles have occurred under the guise of someone attempting so sell an item to passengers in the stopped cars. When the "seller" gets close to the targeted vehicle he attaches an IED, and the target will never know until it goes off. SPECIAL NOTE: Children are often used at traffic control points to sell fruit, newspapers, and other items, or to wash your windshield for a fee. Never open your door or lower your windows—some of these children

What is this child carrying? Could it be an incendiary device to toss at your vehicle?

have received training in how to throw IEDs, grenades, and Molotov cocktails into open vehicles or to shoot drivers. *Do not let a person's age or sex cause you to lower your guard.*

Remember to maintain situational awareness and be alert to what is taking place around you. If you see something placed on or thrown under your vehicle, the only way to counter this is to move the vehicle immediately or exit the vehicle. If you are wearing your seat belt, then that will delay you, so you must look at your threat environment and decide if during low-speed, urban, stop-and-go traffic you need to wear a seat belt—of course, when moving at higher rates of speed you will always wear one.

If You Must Abandon Your Vehicle

If your car is immovable, fully blocked in, or disabled, then you need to disembark and follow through with your preplanned crisis response for that site. If you are traveling in a convoy, observe what is taking place around the vehicles in front of and behind you. If you are in high-profile vehicles and the delay is extended in an urban environment, one security man from each vehicle might want to get out and walk around the vehicle. If you are using deception and traveling in low-profile vehicles, then act like everyone else. Blending in is the best security.

OPEN-BED TRUCKS

Many military and private security companies use open-bed trucks as transportation vehicles overseas. Although they work well for moving cargo, you should do a little preparation before using one as a security vehicle. You will always need someone in the back, in case an attacker decides to set some type of explosive device back there or toss one in as you drive by. You do not want to use tarps or other devices to close this area off, because then you would have an area that you can't search with your eyes, and someone could hide something in there.

The best bet is to enclose the back of your vehicle with chicken wire, using 1 x 1-inch wooden slats in the corners. Make sure that you put chicken wire on top as well. Chicken wire is flexible so it is not hard enough for a Molotov cocktail bottle to break against, and it will keep attackers from tossing anything into the rear of the vehicle. It will not stop security personnel from firing out, so they can still use their weapons with the 1 x 1 boards as support. This also will not stop anyone in the back of the vehicle from exiting, since the boards are easily broken. Chicken wire will also keep the back open so you can see what is back there.

Seats in the back should be installed in the center of the cargo bed facing out to provide a more stable firing platform and to give an increased perception of your security's capabilities. If more protection is needed because of personnel riding in the back, you can set up a wooden frame around the interior of the truck bed. On this frame you can drape Kevlar blankets or spare body armor. This type of material is much lighter than plate steel, and it will not take away from the handling characteristics of the vehicle. Another expedient measure is cutting old rubber tires into strips and placing them on frames around the bed of the truck two or three layers thick. The rubber is lighter than armor and slows down incoming shrapnel and rounds down enough to limit their effectiveness (depending on the type of round).

• • •

A thorough study of interviews with survivors of different types of vehicle ambushes and detailed analyses of the attack sites revealed several common factors in the sequence of events leading up to the attacks.

- The attack was a complete surprise.
- The driver was boxed in before he realized what was happening and was unable to take any type of evasive action.

- When the driver did attempt an evasive maneuver, it was to steer away (move right) from the attackers; doing this merely created more maneuvering room for the attackers to use their weapons.
- Even when they had noticed a car full of people following them in the middle of the day, the people interviewed had not attached any significance to this and thought the attackers were just other people out driving around conducting business.

These facts reinforce what has been emphasized throughout this text: the importance of constant security and observation whenever you are traveling so that you recognize an attack at the earliest possible moment. The sooner you recognize this threat, the sooner you can assess the situation, the location of the threat, and the visible strength of the threat, and then decide what actions to take so that you can escape. Whenever you are in a vehicle, whether it is moving or stopped, remember to do the following:

- Stay alert.
- Drive ahead.
- Maintain adequate distance.
- Maintain the inner or outer lane.
- Be prepared.
- Keep the vehicle under control.
- Keep seat belts fastened.

CHAPTER 14

Motorcade Operations

If you are working in a high-threat area and must travel in more than one vehicle, you need to be familiar with separate considerations and tactics. Multi-vehicle operations take training and practice to do well. You need one front and two rear security vehicles, enough additional vehicles to carry the person or persons you are transporting, and an extra vehicle in case a transport vehicle breaks down or becomes incapacitated.

When traveling, you should vary your speeds to prevent someone from command-detonating a bomb as your vehicles pass. The practice of running your vehicles at extreme speeds (65 mph or more) is dangerous because it makes your vehicles less stable and harder to control, especially armored vehicles and SUVs. Keeping your speeds down to 45–60 mph gives you more stability when driving, which makes it easier to avoid accidents and to recover from receiving partial IED hits, going off road, blowing tires, and having to weave through slower traffic and obstacles that may be on the roadway. Also, whenever one of the three lead vehicles takes damage, these speeds allow the rear security vehicles to slow down and assess what is happening so they can assist. You do not want to pass through the attack area and then have to turn around

and come back for personnel—this increases the danger to everyone.

The people in the lead vehicle should be the most experienced and the best trained in attack recognition, since they will be the first to spot IEDs or other threats, and react. The lead personnel should give directions to the other vehicles for movement purposes. Your rear security vehicles should carry your best shots, since they will be the ones who do most of the firing if an ambush or other type of attack ensues. Vehicles carrying clients or VIPs should have a security driver and the detail commander, who can make decisions based on what is taking place with the lead vehicle when situations arise. The security personnel are also there to get the principal's vehicle out of the area if an attack occurs, or to move the occupants to the backup vehicle if the vehicle is disabled. In Iraq, I have seen vehicles carrying their passengers stop because the security detail wanted to stop and engage the attackers. Do not let cowboys put your life or the life of your client in danger!

Every vehicle should be carrying smoke grenades to help obscure your following vehicles as targets. The reason you want two security vehicles in the rear will be discussed in more detail when I get into specific tac-

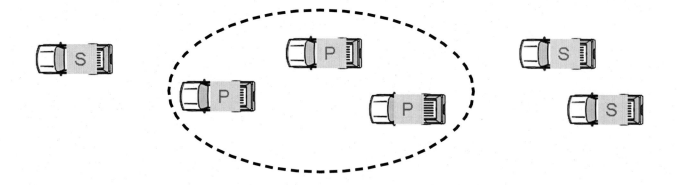

Convoy movement with two passenger vehicles (the third passenger vehicle is really a backup and will move up to block any traffic trying to enter from the sides) and three security vehicles. The idea is to create a protective bubble around the passenger vehicles by having 360-degree observation coverage and preventing any vehicles from passing or pulling up next to the convoy. It also prevents the convoy from passing any vehicle that has not been checked by the lead security vehicle. If there is a vehicle stopped on the road, the lead vehicle will approach and order the occupants away from the vehicle until the convoy passes.

tics, but basically one will provide cover fire and one will recover personnel from vehicles that sustain damage. You never want vehicles that make it through an attack site to have to turn around and come back through it.

Another technique is to use one front and one rear security vehicle, with the principal riding in a third vehicle. This is a good technique for short trips since a backup transport for the principal will probably not be needed, but this forces the rear vehicle to cover all traffic to the rear, including blocking on-ramps and both lanes on a two-lane road. This technique requires a lot of skill and experience to perform well. Every vehicle will have a security person with an automatic weapon in the rear of the vehicle covering the back 180-degree arc of the vehicle. Any vehicle that approaches from the rear is a possible hostile.

While the rear security vehicles will be the first to access and engage any threat from the rear, each vehicle in a motorcade needs to be able to protect itself from an overrun attack while moving, especially in an urban environment with heavy traffic.

Any time your motorcade is attacked, you need to get out of the kill zone and move to a safe haven. You can assess injuries to personnel while on the move. Security personnel can engage if they have a target to shoot at, but no vehicles should stop or turn around, and security personnel should not dismount their vehicles to engage hostiles when all vehicles still have the ability to continue movement or pick up personnel who are stranded.

SCENARIO 1
One of the vehicles is disabled as it passes through an ambush.

Regardless of which vehicle is disabled, unless it is the last security vehicle in the convoy, all vehicles in front of it will continue on. If the vehicle can still be moved, the second security vehicle in the formation will come up behind it and push it out of the kill zone to a safer area for recovery while the third vehicle provides overwatch protection. The driver of the stopped vehicle needs to put the vehicle in neutral and make sure the

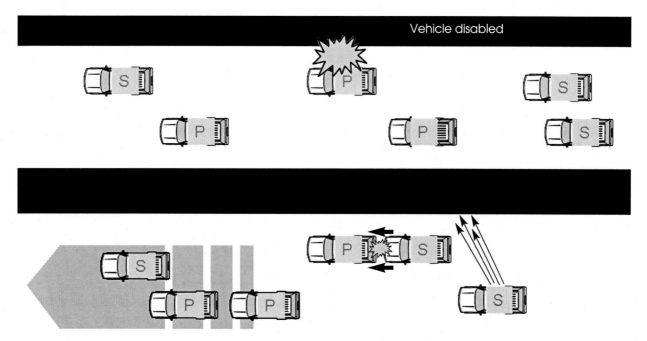

Security vehicle pushes the disabled vehicle out of the kill zone while the second security vehicle provides overwatch. All other vehicles proceed out of the kill zone.

brakes are not engaged. If the driver is incapacitated, someone in the vehicle needs to do this. The driver of the vehicle that will push will call over the radio, "Prepare for impact," to give those occupants who are not incapacitated a chance to prepare themselves. To prepare for impact, the people need to make sure their heads are all the way back in the headrests, and someone needs to steer the vehicle. The driver of the vehicle doing the pushing will do good threshold braking and attempt to strike the vehicle at 10 mph or less. Once contact is made, he will then accelerate and get the vehicle moving out of the attack area as quickly as possible, with the fire-support vehicle following and continuing to engage targets and throw smoke.

Why do you want to push a vehicle in this manner? First, it is easier to move the vehicle filled with people than to recover people who are injured and unconscious while you are under fire. Second, to recover personnel by taking them out of the stopped vehicle will bring the occupants of both vehicles under fire in a planned kill zone. Third, the chances are great that there is more than one IED to

hurt personnel who are assisting or to disable another vehicle. There could be personnel waiting to command-detonate other devices as soon as another vehicle is stopped or personnel are exposed. Fourth, it moves everyone out of the kill zone faster, which is the best way to save lives and get people to aid more quickly.

SCENARIO 2
The hit vehicle cannot be pushed or towed because of damage, and people need to be transferred to another vehicle.

This can happen when the axle on the vehicle is destroyed and the vehicle cannot roll forward, the steering wheel is destroyed so you can't steer, the entire front compartment is destroyed, or basically any circumstance that won't allow the vehicle to roll forward out of the kill zone. The security vehicle that will be acting as the retrieval vehicle needs to start slowing down before entering the kill zone; if necessary, it needs to stop before entering this area. While the damaged vehicle is being dismounted, all other vehicles need to pass through the kill zone and continue on to the safe area, except for the second rear security vehicle, which will pass through the kill zone and set up an overwatch to provide cover fire for the retrieval vehicle. The passengers in the vehicle that was damaged need to start exiting the vehicle on the side that is not taking fire and start throwing smoke. The disabled vehicle will act as a protective barricade during the retrieval operation, and smoke will obscure what is taking place.

All injured personnel must be pulled from the vehicle, and the vehicle commander needs to make sure everyone is out and accounted for. He will then signal the retrieval vehicle to come ahead for pickup. Depending on the condition of the personnel in the damaged vehicle, the retrieval vehicle needs to adjust speed.

The idea is to have the retrieval vehicle roll behind the damaged vehicle and use it as cover, without stopping. The people from the damaged vehicle will then hang onto the retrieval vehicle as it passes, entering through the windows or open doors or just hanging onto an open door. The objective is to get them out of the kill zone as fast as possible, without having another stopped vehicle. Then the retrieval vehicle will continue on at the fastest, safest speed. Once out of the kill zone, it will stop and transfer passengers to the backup vehicle or get everyone inside and move to the nearest safe haven.

Why do you want to recover people in this manner? First, it turns the disabled vehicle into a barricade, providing cover for its passengers as well as for the retrieval vehicle. Second, it prevents your having two stopped vehicles in the kill zone; a moving target is much harder to hit, even if it is only going 5 mph. Third, it is the fastest way to get personnel out of the kill zone so they can get to a safe haven and be treated. Fourth, this allows the second security vehicle to provide cover fire and the security personnel to use smoke

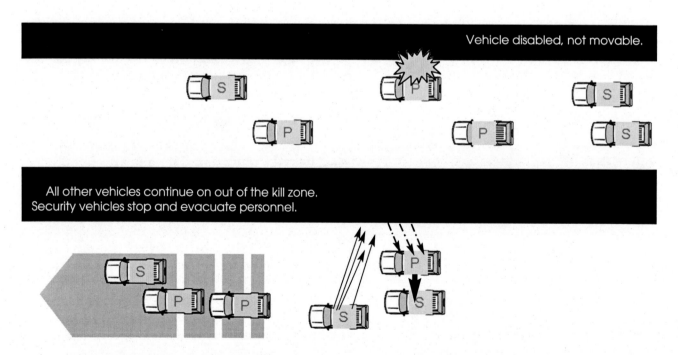

To evacuate, the security vehicle will pull up beside the disabled vehicle, and personnel will be evacuated while keeping the disabled vehicle between them and the incoming fire. All personnel in the disabled vehicle need to exit to the side that is not taking fire. The second security vehicle will provide covering fire if necessary. Once everyone is out of the disabled vehicle, the recovery vehicle will move out, with the security vehicle following.

The worst side from which to attempt retrieval: there are not as many entry points, and it exposes the driver to enemy fire.

The best side from which to attempt retrieval: there are more entry points. No matter on which side retrieval is attempted, people can lie on the hood, hang in the windows, and go in through the back for retrieval.

in the area to obscure targets, as well as providing an element of surprise by keeping the other vehicle back until pickup. Fifth, I have seen pickups attempted where the retrieval vehicle pulls between the disabled vehicle and the firing position. This offers fewer points of entry for those being rescued, and the retrieval vehicle is now taking damage and could be disabled—so instead of one disabled vehicle you could have two. Even an armored vehicle can take only so much punishment

before becoming inoperable—and an armored vehicle does not have armored tires.

SCENARIO 3
The last vehicle is hit, and personnel need to be recovered.

A rescue in these circumstances will be difficult and must be practiced and coordinated. When one of the last vehicles is disabled and you are in contact with the personnel in it, you must decide whether to continue on with the principal or attempt to retrieve stranded personnel.

If you decide to attempt retrieval, then the first security vehicle and the vehicles transporting the clients will continue on to the closest safe haven. The other rear security vehicle and the spare transport vehicle will stop and attempt pickup. The security personnel in the rear vehicle will lay down as much covering fire as possible and start throwing smoke grenades if they have them. After making sure all sensitive items are out of the vehicle and all personnel are accounted for, they will then prepare the vehicle for destruction by puncturing one of the spare gas cans inside the vehicle or punching a hole in the gas tank. The other security vehicle will be laying down covering fire to keep the enemy from engaging the personnel in the disabled vehicle. The alternate transport vehicle will then back at high speed into the kill zone and stop behind the disabled vehicle. The people from the disabled vehicle will evacuate, and then that vehicle will accelerate out of the area. While the recovery vehicle is moving away, the disabled vehicle will be set on fire by the security element. This will cause smoke and confusion, and ensure that the vehicle is not going to be used against a friendly target. The transport vehicle backs in, because the rear of the vehicle can take more damage and this technique keeps the driver on the side opposite the one taking fire.

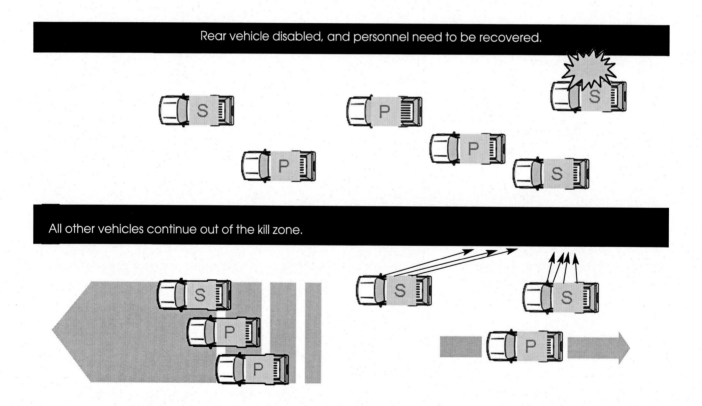

To evacuate personnel, the nondisabled security vehicle will assume an overwatch role and begin laying down cover fire. People in the disabled vehicle will also lay down covering fire. The spare transport vehicle will back at a high speed into the kill zone behind the disabled vehicle and pick up personnel. Once everyone is on board, this vehicle will accelerate out of the kill zone.

SCENARIO 4
Vehicle needs to be towed.

Sometimes there will not be enough warning for the follow vehicle to push the struck vehicle out of the kill zone, and everyone will pass by. When this happens, you will have to do a towing operation. This is not as difficult or time consuming as it sounds, since all vehicles that you use will be prepared for towing before they are ever driven on an operation.

When all the vehicles have passed by, the rear security vehicles will stop. One vehicle will provide covering fire and smoke, and the other one will do the towing. The vehicle towing will reverse to the disabled vehicle, where a person from the disabled vehicle will be out waiting, using the front wheels and engine block as cover. When the recovery vehicle comes to a stop, the waiting passenger will run up, grab the tow strap, and hook it through the towing hook attached to the front of the disabled vehicle.

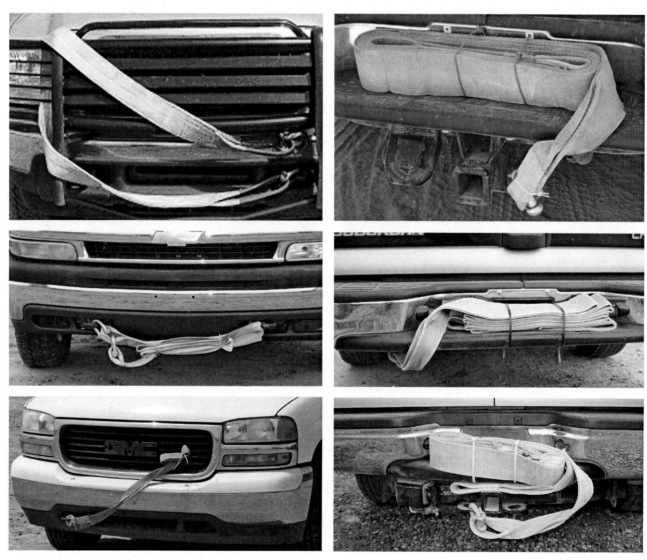

Vehicles rigged with front tow strap.　　　　Vehicles rigged with rear tow strap.

Trucks in a convoy with prerigged tow straps.

You should never rig your tow strap so that you have to break the integrity of the vehicle's protection to get it out and use it. You do not want to be opening doors in the kill zone to get at a strap when it is needed.

He will then reenter the disabled vehicle as the recovery vehicle starts forward, towing the disabled vehicle out of the kill zone. Vehicle movement can take place within 5 seconds of the towing vehicle's starting to move backward.

This type of operation depends entirely on having all your vehicles prerigged for towing operations and conducting rehearsals for all personnel to practice hooking up the towing straps and towing a vehicle. Practice makes these operations run smoother and faster.

To prerig your vehicle, a tow strap that will pull twice the weight of your heaviest vehicle is needed for *every vehicle*. The tow strap is attached at the rear of each vehicle to a frame strong point; then the tow strap is layered across the rear bumper. Each layer needs to be held in place with string or 40-pound cotton webbing. You can also use zip ties, but they are not strong enough to stop someone from pulling the tow strap out for use. Also be aware that when they get hot, zip ties can slide out, depending on the tension placed on them. Do not use tape or rubber bands to secure the strap; these degrade with heat, and your tow strap might fall and be dragged. You want to be able to pull the end of the tow strap loose with just your hands.

The end of the tow strap needs to be prerigged with a hook that has a closing hasp. The front of every vehicle needs to have an eyehole rigged or a towing cable or some other type of tow point that is permanently attached and easily available. This allows someone to run to the back of one vehicle, pull the strap loose, and snap it on in less than 5 seconds. Prerigging your vehicles in

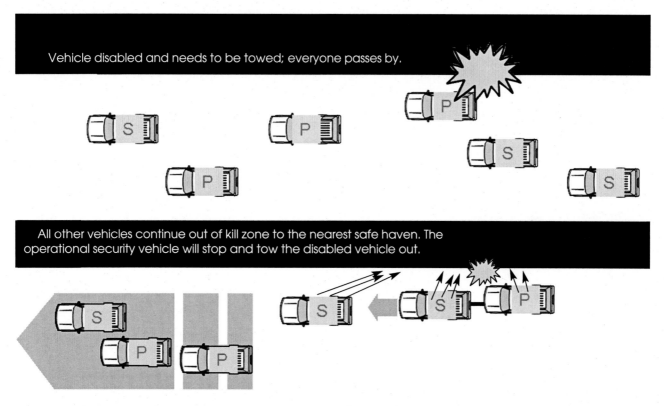

To evacuate, the security vehicle will pull in front of the disabled vehicle and then back up to it. The person on the nonfiring side will exit and take the tow strap already in place and hook it to the disabled vehicle. As soon as it is hooked up, the nondisabled vehicle will start pulling the disabled one out of the kill zone. All personnel still able to perform will provide covering fire.

Vehicle is down, and security personnel are trying to make it movable for towing in the middle of nowhere.

this manner will make your tow hookup times so quick that you will catch the ambushers off guard.

SCENARIO 5
Vehicles have to stop for nonmechanical reasons.

This can happen when you are traveling through areas where there is a lot of livestock and the roads are used to move it. Make sure you have a loud horn or an air horn in each vehicle. The first security vehicle should let everyone know what is coming up so they can prepare.

All the vehicles need to slow down so the first vehicle can create a space to drive through, but it is important not to stop any of the vehicles. If only a narrow space exists, then the two rear security vehicles need to pull up and station themselves on opposite sides of the road, looking out to provide cover if necessary as the vehicles make their way through the obstruction of livestock.

If enemy contact is made, then just drive. It doesn't matter how many animals you hit or how badly you hurt them—just get out of the area as soon as possible. You can always find out the number of animals hurt or killed and send restitution to the owner later. Remember to strike animals just as you would a car—aim for the head or the rear part of the animal. This will push it out of the way and cause less damage to your vehicle. Hitting an animal head-on, especially a large animal, can hurt people inside the vehicle; damage the radiator, battery, or windshield; or activate the air bags or fuel-cutoff switches. Also, driving over the top of a large animal can cause your tires to lose traction, slowing or stopping you.

SCENARIO 6
Road barricade, vehicle ambush.

This can happen when there is a random barricade set up to catch any foreigners or other people considered high-value targets. It can involve no vehicle, a single vehicle, or multiple vehicles, and it can be there to extort tolls from travelers; steal vehicles, weapons, or equipment; or kill specific or random targets.

The thing to remember is that you want to do everything you can to avoid this scenario. When the lead vehicle observes this type of operation to the front, he will radio what is going on to all vehicles and start slowing down, looking for a good place to turn around and leave. The two rear security vehicles will move to the front of the formation to pull security overwatch on the barricade and prevent anyone from coming out or firing on the convoy. The lead security vehicle will get everyone turned around and start moving out in a safe direction. When he is rolling again, he will radio the two rear vehicles, which will then fall back into formation.

If the ambush or barricade gets put in place after the lead vehicle has already passed, then someone from that vehicle will call back and notify the rest of the vehicles what is taking place. The next vehicle in line will find a place and turn around; one of the rear security vehicles will take the lead and move the passenger vehicles out of the area. The other rear security vehicle will move and take up an overwatch position on the barricade while the lead vehicle makes it back to the formation. If at any time people manning the barricade take a threatening posture, or any vehicle that has already passed is being interfered with, then both security vehicles will fire on the barricade until all vehicles are back in the convoy. Do what is needed to stay together.

SCENARIO 7
Vehicle accident.

I discussed accidents in detail in the last chapter, so here I will just summarize what to do if one of your vehicles is in an accident or if you come upon the scene of an accident.

Accidents are going to happen wherever you go, in both urban and rural environ-ments. The thing to do is keep going. Regardless of the type of accident, if all your vehicles are operational, continue on. Report the accident and pay restitution later as required, including covering medical bills and fixing the vehicles involved if you are the cause of the accident. If the accident is not connected with any of your vehicles, then pass by if possible; if you cannot, turn around and find another route.

I have seen several security details whose members wanted to get out and ren-der assistance. This is a very bad idea—it's not their job or yours. Unless you saw the accident happen, you have no way of know-ing if it is real. Even if you saw it happen or your vehicles are involved, you have no way of knowing whether the accident was planned. Have laminated cards made up with your company's or organization's con-tact number, address, and other information, and drop one at the site so people will know whom to contact.

You are not there to render any type of assistance. Your security detail is not there to work as nurses or ambulance drivers. The safety and security of your convoy is the only thing you should be concerned with, and getting you, your people, or your family to their destination as safely as possible is your only goal.

SCENARIO 8
Overrun attack from the rear.

This type of attack has been used for a while in Europe and Asia and is becoming more common around the world. It occurs when the threat attacks your vehicle while you are en route to a primary area. These types of attacks can be made from any type of platform: bicycle, motorcycle, car, van, or truck. As discussed previously, these attacks are difficult to defeat.

When traveling in a convoy, everyone needs to keep their eyes up and moving around, observing their surroundings, includ-ing looking to the rear for any signs of possible attack or hostile intent. The two rear

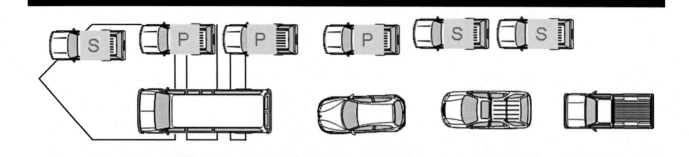

Urban traffic can be very limiting to a convoy or motorcade. The motorcade should use both sides of the street in the direction of travel.

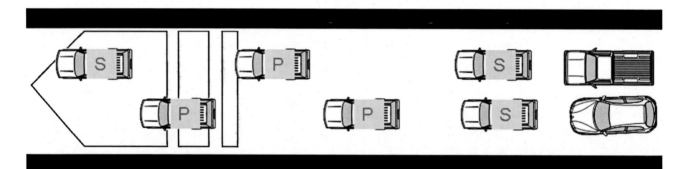

By using both sides of the street when moving slowly in urban traffic, the motorcade retains greater control of the environment and takes its vehicles out of alignment, making them much harder to hit.

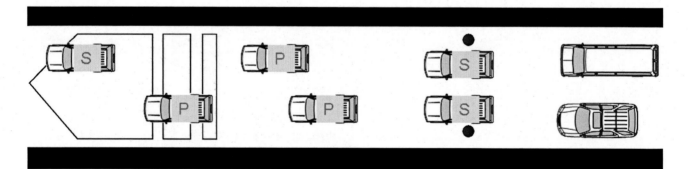

In slow or stopped traffic, having a man from the rear security vehicles open his door and step out, either on the street or the running board, and pull security can be very intimidating to others, especially to those with hostile intent. Plus, it increases the security agent's field of view.

security vehicles are extremely important in all these scenarios, but especially in defeating the overrun attack from the rear. All vehicles approaching from the rear are regarded as hostile; it doesn't matter whether you are in urban or rural movement or the type of vehicle that is approaching (e.g., emergency vehicles or taxicabs, military vehicles, SUVs, school buses). There have been reports of all these types of vehicles being stolen and used in attacks. You need to watch all of them carefully, with your weapons locked and loaded and ready for use.

If someone attempts to pass the vehicles in the motorcade, whether it is stopped or moving, the two rear security vehicles need to block the roadway and prevent any vehicle, two-wheel or four-wheel, from passing until it is confirmed friendly. In really slow-moving or stopped urban traffic, you can have a person from the two rear security vehicles get out and walk alongside with their doors open and weapons on. Sometimes a visible deterrent will make people think twice before attempting an attack. This sounds easy, but, once again, preconceived notions of who a bad guy is always come into play.

I witnessed a security detail doing a great job denying access to everyone except U.S. soldiers and authorized contractors . . . until two schoolgirls came by on a motor scooter. Then the security guys just smiled, waved, and let the scooter pass. When I confronted the detail leader about what happened, he basically replied that "they were only girls." My jaw hit the floor, and I took him back to the office and showed him the 27 attacks against Westerners that had been orchestrated by females around the world. You and your security detail have to get over the notion that females and children are not a threat. Such ignorance can get you killed.

SCENARIO 9
Overrun attack from the front.

This is the same type of attack as in scenario 8, but here the attacker fires on you as he passes along the length of the convoy or motorcade from the front to the rear. With this type of attack, you can do little to prepare or counter, but personnel in the lead security vehicle need to keep their eyes open for any attack indicators, so that as much warning as possible can be passed to the other vehicles.

Although nothing can be done to prevent this type of attack, the two rear security vehicles can stop it quickly after it has started. After reporting that an overrun attack from the front is taking place, the driver of the lead vehicle will pick up speed, pushing vehicles out of the way as necessary to gain speed for the convoy. The two rear security vehicles will then move over: one will cross into the lane of oncoming traffic; the other will take a position in the nearest lane of traffic and continue in the same direction of travel as the convoy. Both security vehicles will engage the attacking vehicle. The driver of the attack vehicle will be unsure of himself and what to do when the one security vehicle crosses into his lane of travel. The other security vehicle can fire as necessary as it passes, marking the target for the other security vehicle as it fires on and attempts to disable the attacker.

Whether the attacker is disabled or destroyed, none of the convoy vehicles should stop as long as none of your vehicles are disabled. The security vehicle will cross over after it has distracted and fired on the attacker, ultimately catching up to the convoy and blocking the rear as necessary. The convoy will have continued on toward a safe haven, with the front security vehicle leading the way and putting as much distance as possible between the attacker and the convoy vehicles. Once they reach a safe haven, they will report the incident to the proper authorities.

SCENARIO 10
Vehicle stops for mechanical reasons.

This is bound to happen sometime to any detail or driver. It is very important to keep your vehicles in top form by performing all scheduled maintenance and doing daily and weekly checks. If one of your vehicles stops during transport because of mechanical failure, then the passengers need to be transferred to the backup vehicle and you need to continue on. Don't forget to lock the vehicle before you leave; you don't want to make it easy for someone to vandalize or destroy it. When it is safe to do so, call someone to recover the vehicle you left behind.

If you are in a high-threat situation without a backup vehicle, you may need to commandeer a vehicle, a taxicab, or another type of vehicle. Move all the occupants into it, take the driver of the commandeered vehicle with you, and leave the area immediately for the closest safe haven. You take the driver of the vehicle with you so you can pay him and explain why you did what you did. Apologize and send him away happy.

Now, this brings up another point: use common sense when you commandeer someone's car. Plenty of people will give you a ride; you don't have to take over a vehicle with an entire family in it or a school bus. Choose a single-occupant vehicle big enough to hold everyone, stop it, ask the driver to get in the back or move over, put everyone in, and leave.

The key, once again, is to keep moving, not to try to fix your vehicle in the middle of a hostile area. So keep all passengers in the car until you get another vehicle, transfer them to it, and *leave* the area.

SCENARIO 11
Changing a tire.

At some time you will probably have to change a tire while in transit. The first thing to think about is why it went flat at that particular time. If you don't know, you need to consider the type of area you are in before stopping your vehicle or vehicles and getting out to change the tire. It is safest for you to adjust your speed, inform everyone of why you have slowed down, and continue driving on the rim. You can drive a long way on the rim, as we have seen many times with police chase scenes on the evening news. While running on a rim, you cannot conduct extreme evasive maneuvers or move at high speeds, but you can keep moving.

Don't worry about the rubber on the tire or the rim, because you should have multiple sets of wheels, tires, and rims ready for use in your vehicle, at your work site, and at your home. Just keep your speed down and steer smoothly, and you will be fine. If you try to maintain a high rate of speed or begin jerking on the wheel, you could cause the rims to dig into the road surface, making the vehicle flip. As emphasized earlier, getting driver training and knowing your vehicle's capabilities are very important for whoever is driving. Also have Fix-A-Flat in your vehicles; a can of that might seal the tire enough that you won't have to change it until you reach your destination.

I have seen security details block a road to all traffic so they can change a tire. This always draws a big crowd of angry people who are trying to use the road and makes you and everyone with you a target of opportunity. It is better to drive on a rim than do this.

MOVEMENT AT NIGHT

Moving at night can be difficult in the best of circumstances, but when traveling in high-threat areas you should consider doing certain things to increase your motorcade's chances of success.

Spotlights

Most vehicles have standard headlights, and most have those headlights placed in the same manner. Depending on the environment you are working in and the number of IEDs your vehicle passes through, your standard headlights probably are not going to last too long. You need to modify your vehicles' lights.

Each vehicle in the convoy should have a 3-million-candlepower spotlight mounted on the top of the vehicle in such a way that it

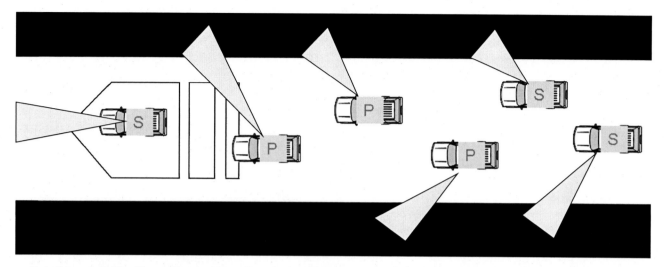

Running at night with spotlights of 2 to 3 million candlepower and no other lights shining will provide enough light to see by and destroy the night vision of anyone who gets caught in the light. Also it will cause people to duck and cover their eyes, making it more difficult for them to time movement and aim weapons. Your convoy could also run with only the security vehicles using their spotlights and the passenger vehicles running dark.

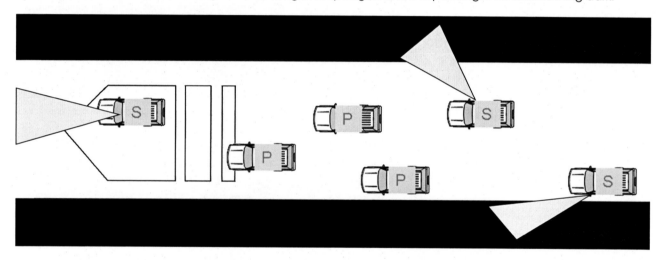

can be turned and manipulated from the passenger compartment. When running at night, these spotlights should be the only lights used on the vehicles, not running lights or regular headlights. The lead vehicle's floodlight should be facing forward, illuminating as much of the roadway as possible. All the vehicles following the lead car should have their lights aimed at the side of the roadway, illuminating the areas surrounding the roads.

This gives you several advantages. First, it should produce enough ambient light for the driver to see well enough to stay on the road. Second, the lights shining to the side of the road will take away the night vision of any potential ambushers and make it harder to time the speed at which you are traveling and almost impossible to aim a weapon or to set off a remote detonation at the right time. Lights used in this manner give many false impressions to those watching them. Fourth, the physiological effect of having a light coming at you while you are trying to ambush someone from the darkness will give any potential attackers something to think about and can cause them to flinch or duck down seeking cover.

Tracers

As far as ammunition goes, the first magazine or belt used at night should have tracers. Tracers have a tremendous psychological effect on people who think they are invisible in the dark. When tracers start coming at them, they will flinch, duck, and maybe even run.

• • •

Many things can happen to you and the vehicle during movement. Attacks are usually the major cause of concern, but traffic accidents can kill you just as easily and are far more common. The vehicles on the right were all involved in accidents. The first was caused by an IED that made the driver lose control of his vehicle and roll it. In the second, the driver just lost control of his vehicle. The driver of the last vehicle wasn't paying attention and got "teed" at an intersection.

CHAPTER 15

Vehicle Bomb Searches

You need to search your vehicles for bombs for several reasons. The first thing that pops into everyone's mind is to find bombs. While this is one of the reasons, it is not the main one. The most important reason for doing a vehicle bomb search is *you want to be seen doing it*. This will raise your overall security profile in the eyes of any surveillance agents. And, as we've learned, most attacks, either criminal or terrorist, take place after surveilling the target. By raising your security profile, you may well be taken off the target list.

When should you do a car bomb search? You should do one every time your vehicle is left unattended (even if just for a bathroom or refreshment break) in an unsecured area. But even if you leave the vehicle in a secure area—unless it is under direct observation of a guard from your own country, not one from the host nation—you should still search it. You can never search too often. Remember, it's your life, your client's life, or the lives of your family members you are protecting.

How long should a search take? One should take between 5 and 15 minutes. I know this doesn't sound like a lot of time, but as Americans we are very time-conscious. If a task takes longer than 15 minutes, most

people will blow it off, especially when they are running late or a vehicle is out in bad weather. Because of the limited amount of time you have, everyone in your family or security detail should also become familiar with all the family or business vehicles. This will help you when you do your search, and it will help your family recognize when things are out of place.

A two-man inspection team will provide a more thorough and efficient search than a solo search. Just be sure that the person who is helping has been trained in what to look for. One person will work to the left and the other to the right, each starting from the center front of the vehicle. Each will also conduct a thorough search of what the other has covered, and both complete the search at the starting point, making two 360-degree walks around the vehicle. Each person should communicate with the other when he finds something he is not sure belongs on or near the vehicle or when he opens a flap or a door. This allows the second searcher to move away from the vehicle in the event of an explosion. The communication also allows people not familiar with the vehicle to get input from someone who is.

There are ways to prepare your vehicle to make it more difficult for bombs or other devices to be planted without detection and to make the search go more quickly for you. The precautions you take at the *end* of each trip before you leave your vehicle can make your next pretrip inspection much easier and more effective.

When possible, park on a hard surface away from any shrubbery and landscaping. When you park on a soft surface—such as grass, sand, or mud—you need to realize that these areas can be tampered with by someone either putting something underneath your tires or running wires or explosives to your vehicle and covering them up. You should also avoid parking near anything that could hide an explosive device, especially if the device is portable.

When you get out of your vehicle, walk around it and pick up all the debris before you leave. If the area is clean when you leave, then you will know when something has been placed near your vehicle, and it will be easier to spot any signs of tampering or bomb trash (e.g., cut or shaved wires or plastic wire coating, tape). Also if you must park by shrubbery or landscaping, walk through it and look for any piles of debris or leaves. Make sure you kick through all those piles and pick up any litter so that any new debris will be obvious when you return and do another walkaround.

I will discuss other ways to make your vehicle more difficult to tamper with after we discuss how to perform a detailed search of a vehicle.

CONDUCTING A SEARCH

Conducting a search is basically the same for all types of vehicles; you just need to fine-tune it for the vehicles you have. I will outline inspection procedures in detail for sedans; then I will outline how the search differs for vans and SUVs, noting things that are unique to each type of vehicle.

Was this debris there when you parked the car? If so, you should not have parked there, or you should have documented what was there before you left. If it was not there, you should be wary of it. It could hide an explosive device.

You should avoid parking in soft areas where someone can hide a device under your tires or hide wires leading from a device to your vehicle.

Undisturbed tread pattern.

Tread pattern that has been disturbed.

A thorough search of any vehicle consists of checking the following areas:

- Perimeter
- Front
- Side one
- Rear
- Opposite side
- Bottom

- Interior
- Under the hood
- Trunk or storage compartment

Sedans

Perimeter

Before you even get to the vehicle, you should always take 5 to 10 minutes to

PERIMETER BOMB SEARCH

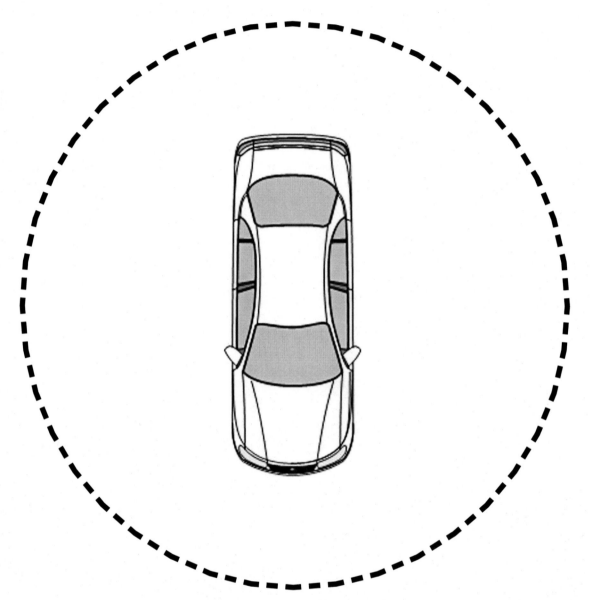

When doing a perimeter search, walk around the area immediately surrounding the vehicle in a 10-foot radius or to the closest area where a device may be hidden. Pay close attention to shrubbery and landscaping.

observe the vehicle, the area from which you will be leaving, and the initial route for as far as you can see. Look for anything out of the ordinary, such as objects that look out of place or that are suspiciously near your vehicles. Also notice if there are any people sitting in cars or congregating in unusual areas. You want to do this search before you leave your office and your resi-

dence. If you have a garage, check the garage door for anything that might have been attached to it, such as a trip wire or other device, before opening it and proceeding out for the day.

The perimeter inspection, or walkaround, is done the same regardless of the type of vehicle. Observe the vehicle and the area immediately surrounding it for about 10 feet

Dumpsters are very convenient places to hide explosive devices, especially when they are placed near parking areas. Avoid parking near them whenever possible, and remind someone in authority that trash receptacles should be placed outside the parking areas and away from all buildings.

These types of easily movable traffic cones are so common in all areas that most people tend to ignore them, especially in parking lots and garages. Any number of different types of explosive devices could be placed inside one of these cones. Stay away!

Movable trash containers can hide a huge quantity of explosives, and people tend to ignore them as well.

or to the closest area where a device may be hidden in such things as shrubbery or landscaping. You are checking for signs of tampering in the dirt or shrubbery if it is close to your vehicle. Directly around your vehicle you are looking for bomb litter lying on the ground. IEDs may either be set off by the victim in some way or command-detonated by someone observing you. When you do your first perimeter check, look for people who are paying an unusual amount of attention to what you are doing. If you notice something unusual about where you parked your vehicle, or just sense that something is wrong or that the vehicle is not the way you left it, leave the vehicle, move to a safe area, and call the authorities. More than likely, the police will arrive first to investigate. If they find a device, they will call EOD personnel. Your life or the life of a family member or client is a high price to pay for complacency.

A word of warning is in order that applies to any area that you search: *Never put your hands anywhere you haven't cleared with your eyes first!*

Front

Once you have completed your search of the area around the sedan, move to the front of the vehicle and visually divide it in half lengthwise.

Inspect the grill for scratches in the paint or on the chrome if the grill is metal, or for busted ribs or paint if it is plastic. Look inside the grill for wires that shouldn't be there or for any other type of material placed behind it that is new. Next, look underneath and behind the front bumper.

Also look closely into the hood area and around the front of the hood where someone could force entry. You are looking for scratched or chipped paint, dents in the metal, or parts of the grill being broken and put back. You should also look at the latch to see if you can find any scratches on it where someone tried to reach in with a tool and pop it open.

Side

Move to one side of the vehicle (it doesn't matter which side you start with) and look at your tires (front and rear) where they make

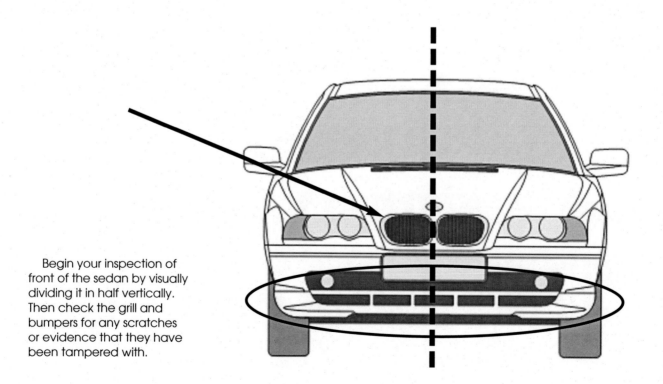

Begin your inspection of front of the sedan by visually dividing it in half vertically. Then check the grill and bumpers for any scratches or evidence that they have been tampered with.

contact with the ground. You are looking for newly turned dirt or a break in the tread pattern in the soil if you were forced to park on dirt or a sandy-type surface. A disturbance in the soil or pattern could indicate that a pressure or pressure-release firing device was placed under your tires.

When you inspect the door to the gas tank for tampering, you are looking for chipped or scratched paint around the front of the door where entry could be forced. Of course, you should have a locking cap on the vehicle so that a bomb or other incendiary device cannot be dropped into the gas tank. After all, gasoline is already an explosive; it just needs to be set off.

Once you have inspected the door and got it open, check the gas cap for possible tampering. Anytime you leave the vehicle, always place a hidden mark on the gas cap and leave it in a certain position (e.g., 2 o'clock). When you return and do your inspection, check to see if the mark is in the original position; if it is not, you will know that someone has tampered with the gas cap. This should be the first time you

actually touch the vehicle during the search. Be cautious of new vehicles that have electronic gas cap releases, which supply the terrorist with an electric power source that he can use. Also avoid gas door releases in the passenger compartment, which pass under the vehicle, because some can be popped open with a pair of needle-nose pliers.

Examine the window and the weather stripping for signs of forcible entry. Look to see whether the paint is chipped or scratched or there are dents in the frame that suggest that something was placed to apply pressure. Be sure to check the weather stripping for tears or cuts, which could be signs of a coat hanger, Slim Jim, or some other device being used to force entry into the vehicle.

Be very observant of the door locks and the door handles or unlock buttons to see if material around these areas has been scratched or scraped by an object. When inspecting the door lock, look for scratches and nicks on the pull knob, but also look at the bezel at the bottom of the knob to make sure it is still in place.

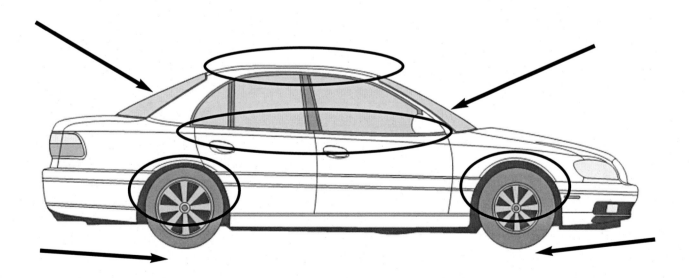

When conducting a side inspection of a sedan, look around the tires and inside the wheel wells, the windows and weather stripping, and the doors and handles for evidence of tampering. Also look inside the vehicle to see if any suspicious package or person is inside.

Look inside the passenger compartment for any new objects that may have been placed there, for any other signs of tampering, and for people who may be hiding in your vehicle.

Rear

Next, move on to the rear. Check the trunk for signs of forced entry. Check the opening of the exhaust pipe for signs of a device. A screen mesh welded over the exhaust pipe opening or bolts inserted through the exhaust pipe and welded in place will prevent devices from being placed in it. Be extra vigilant when checking the bottom and sides of the gas tank, because the gas tank is generally the most explosive area of the vehicle. Small soap-dish charges are easily concealed and difficult to detect.

Continue to the other side of the vehicle and follow the same procedures as for side one. As you inspect the side and rear of the vehicle, also examine the entire exhaust pipe, the muffler, and the drive shaft for devices, especially around the universal joints. When you return to the front of the vehicle, inspect the other side of the front grill and the bumper.

Side Two

Move on to the opposite side of the vehicle and inspect it just as you did the first side.

Bottom

Next you need to check the bottom of the vehicle and along the sides of the gas tank. As explained earlier, the gas tank is already an explosive device that just needs a trigger, which makes it a favorite target for terrorists. Look at the tank itself for any additions or attachments. Also check the bolts holding the tank for scratches or clean areas where they have been loosened recently. Next look on top of the gas tank. There is usually a space of 1 to 3 inches between the tank and the underside of the body, so be very observant when checking these areas. *Remember, the gas tank is generally the most explosive area of the vehicle.*

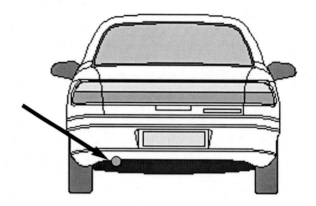

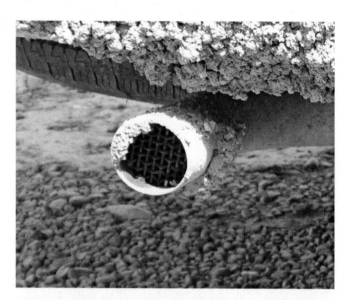

During the rear inspection, check the tailpipe carefully for emplaced devices. Better yet, place screen mesh over or a screw through the tailpipe to prevent a device from being placed in the tailpipe.

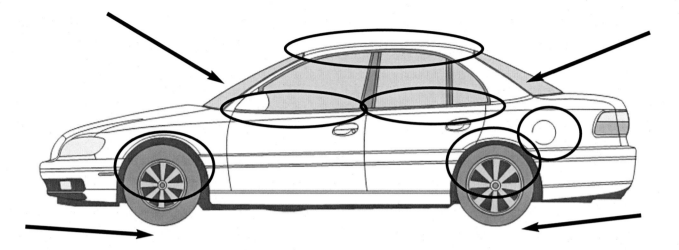

Perform the same inspection on the second side as you did on the first, paying close attention to the tires, the gas tank, doors, windows, weather stripping, and passenger compartment.

As part of your interior inspection, open the door slightly to check the seam. If no signs of tampering are evident, slowly open the door more widely and continue your inspection until the door is completely open.

Be sure to check on top of any area where a device can be placed, including the drive shaft, muffler, and frame. Get to know the underside of your vehicle so you can tell when things have been altered or added.

Interior

You are now ready to actually enter your vehicle. But, first, check the door locks for scratches or any other type of damage or forcible entry. If the vehicle was locked when you left it and unlocked when you returned, then something is wrong. *Do not get inside.*

Next, look inside the vehicle windows, making sure that all the preparation work you did is still good: compartments open, headrests undisturbed, and visors still visible. Observe the opposite door for strange objects or wires. You can look in either of the side windows as well as through the windshield. In some models you can look through the windshield and see almost to the rear seat. When looking inside a door, you may be able to see all the way to the floorboard. Do not touch the vehicle or lean on it; this could cause a tremor switch to function.

Once you determine that nothing is wrong with the interior, closely examine the door, especially the seam where the door meets the body. Look for wires or objects attached to the door from the inside. Next, open the door slightly. Using your mirror and flashlight, continue to inspect the seam. Repeat this procedure until the door is completely open.

Next, inspect the rearview mirror and headrests to ensure that they have not been replaced with IEDs or had IEDs inserted in them. Check the position of the sun visors. Remember, whenever you leave the vehicle, make sure the visors are in the down position so that no device can be emplaced and hidden from your view during inspection. To save time during your searches, remember to always leave the glove compartment, ashtrays, and any other compartments open and empty. Consider removing these hide sites, if you never use them, from the interior of your vehicle.

Next, look under the dashboard. You will not be able to identify every single wire, but you should know the general features and be able to determine whether someone has planted an IED or added wires. If possible, tape or flex-band as many of the wires together as you can reach; that way you will have a much better chance of noticing a wire

The interior of this car is ready for preentry inspection: it is free of debris, and the compartments are empty and open.

Before entering the vehicle, check the positioning of the rearview mirror, headrests, and sun visors to make sure nothing has been hidden in them.

Open the hood slightly and check the seam before opening completely and checking under the hood.

Check under the insulation or, better yet, remove it so it isn't used to hide explosive or incendiary devices.

Today's engines are very complicated. You need to take the time to learn what your engine looks like to spot anything suspicious.

that has been added. And don't forget, you can always mark the wires to know when a new one has been added.

As you move on to inspect the front seat, be especially careful not to put your hands anywhere you cannot see is clear, and do not lean or rest your hands on any part of the vehicle, including the seats. Use the same procedures for opening the other doors as described earlier. As you inspect the rear seat, check the front seat again, looking from the rear toward the front.

As noted, keeping your vehicle's interior clean and free of debris makes it harder to hide a device in your vehicle, which will simplify your search.

Under the Hood

Many late-model vehicles have a hood release in the interior. If your vehicle does not, install locks on the hood.

Before you actually release the hood latch, have a second person hold the hood down to prevent it from snapping up before the second hood latch engages. This jolt is often enough to trigger a tremor or mercury switch or allow a pressure-release trigger to fire. If you are alone, place a heavy object (10 to 15 pounds) on top of the hood to hold it down or release the spring tension so the hood doesn't pop up and needs to be lifted. Once the hood has been released from the inside, slowly raise it and check around the seam as you did the doors.

Look for unusually clean wires that contrast with dirty wires in the engine compartment. Count the spark plug wires to determine whether an extra wire has been attached. You should mark the wires under the hood just as you did those under the dash with paint or fingernail polish. You are also checking for clean areas, where things have been touched or added. Most engine compartments will have the same level of oily dirt all over.

Check the inside of the air cleaner. Make the same type of mark on the air cleaner that you did on the gas cap. When you check it, look for signs of tampering.

Inspect the exhaust manifold for thermal switches and then check along the firewall, which is a common place for planting a device, since the engine will force most of the blast back into the passenger compartment, and there is not much reinforcement between the engine and the passenger compartment. Conversely, a bomb placed on the front of the engine block will have part of its force deflected away from the victim.

Trunk

Before opening the trunk, inspect along the seam. But be especially observant at the bottom and by the lock, because these are the places where you need to break the seam to force open the trunk. Hold the trunk down as you turn the key to prevent an initial spring. Crouch down so that you can look into the trunk and see any wires or IEDs. Remember to sweep your eyes along the entire length of the bottom seam and from front to back along the rear seat. A flashlight can be of great assistance.

Following the same opening procedures you used for the hood, open the trunk completely. Many vehicles have deep wells by the rear quarter panels that make excellent spaces for IEDs. You must also carefully inspect the spare tire area and check the partition separating the trunk from the rear passenger seat. A small soap-dish charge could be employed very effectively, since only wire springs, padding, and the upholstery of the seat separate the trunk from the rear seat. Mark the spare tire in advance the same way as you did the gas cap and air cleaner and see if it has been touched. Don't forget to check the spare tire's air pressure to make sure it has not been tampered with.

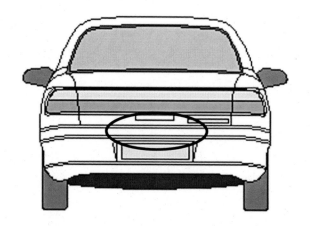

To inspect the trunk of your sedan, check around the opening for signs of forcible entry, and open the trunk lid slightly and peer inside before opening fully, and look under the covering at the top and around the seams.

Vans

Inspecting a van is much the same as for a sedan: perimeter, side one, front, side two, rear, bottom, and interior. But there are some special considerations with vans as well. A van is generally larger and has more areas in which to stash a bomb, including the wheel well. With a van you don't have a trunk, but you have the back door, the storage compartment, and more windows and window stripping to inspect.

Rear

As well as looking at all the areas discussed under the sedan search, you are checking the back doors of the van for signs of forced entry. So look along the seams near where the door latch is located for chipped paint, scratched metal, or for indentations where someone has placed something to apply pressure and force the doors open. You also need to check the lock itself and the surrounding area for scratches, and you will check the rear windows for signs, just as you checked the other windows of the vehicle.

On all vehicles, you have to do a thorough search of gas tank and the area around it because it is a favorite target for saboteurs. But on vans you must be extra vigilant because of the extra space, usually 1 to 3 inches, between the tank and the underside of the body.

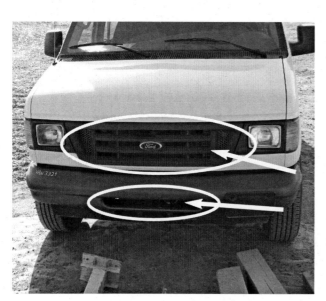

Begin your van inspection as you would for a sedan. After checking the perimeter, move to the front of the van. Inspect the grill for scratches in the paint or on the chrome if the grill is metal or for busted ribs or paint if it is plastic. Look inside the grill for wires that shouldn't be there or for any other type of material placed behind it that is new. Next, look underneath and behind the front bumper.

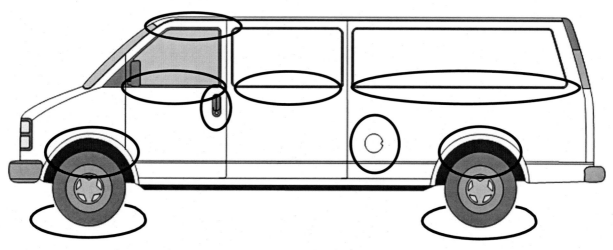

A side inspection of a van includes the windows, weather stripping, gas cap, tires, and wheel wells.

As part of your side inspection, check the terrain around the tires to see if there is evidence of activity around the vehicle. Also check the wheel wells for a bomb or signs of tampering.

A critical part of your side inspection is to check the gas cap to see if anyone has tried to tamper with it. You should have a locking gas cap so no one can get inside to emplace a bomb or other incendiary device in the gas tank.

Front and side windows of a passenger van need to be checked carefully for signs of forced entry.

When inspecting the back of the van, look for signs of attempted entry: scratched metal, chipped paint, gaps in the weather stripping, or anything else that looks suspicious.

These are just a few places underneath a van where a device can be placed; you should know them all.

Bottom

In addition to the bottom areas discussed under sedans, on vans you need to check the spare tire, which is usually located underneath the rear end of the vehicle. Check the tire pressure to make sure the tire still has air in it and hasn't been replaced. Look at the mounting hardware for signs of recent use, and be sure to look on top of the tire to see if anything has been placed up there. If possible, use a chain and lock assembly to secure the tire to the vehicle.

The tailpipe is a favorite place to stash a bomb. To prevent this, place a screw through or a mesh screen over the tailpipe.

On a van, the spare tire is mounted underneath the rear end. Check it for any signs of tampering.

Interior

The problem with inspecting the interior of vans from the outside is that they sit too high up to effectively see along the door surface of the window you are looking in. Also the dash is too high and too close to see along the closer side of the doors. These present problems during this phase of the inspection. Follow the other interior inspection steps outlined for sedans.

Make marks with a pen or fingernail polish along the seams of the sun visors and on the mirror to alert you if they have been replaced or altered.

You need to check the fuse assembly, located at the end of the dash, before departure. Use tape or fingernail polish to mark the seam area so you can tell if someone has opened this compartment.

Under the dash, check the carpet and floor mats, which can be used to hide explosives. Ideally, you should have removed the mats and cut the carpet off at the bottom of the pedals to make it hard to hide anything here.

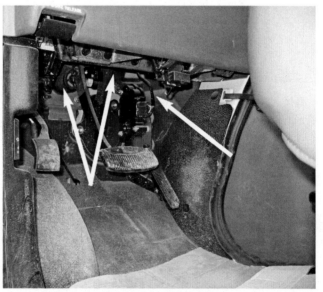

You can't know all the wires under the dash, but you should have a good idea of what is generally there and be able to spot any additions or alterations. You should tape or tie the wires together and mark each wire to tip you off to any tampering.

Before opening the hood, you need to check it for any devices that could have been attached magnetically, as well as for trip wires leading from the underside of the hood to the device.

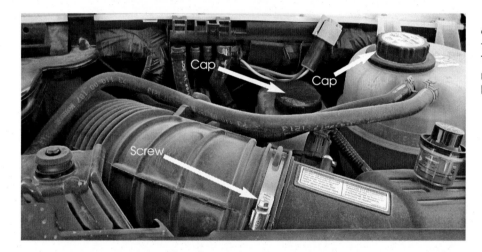

Use paint or fingernail polish on screws and caps to mark the positions you left them in. That way, if the mark has been moved, you know someone has been in that compartment.

An explosive device needs a power source, so check very carefully under the hood for any new or altered wires. Also look at the battery terminals and the electric fan motor for any new or unusual wires or to see if they appear cleaner than usual.

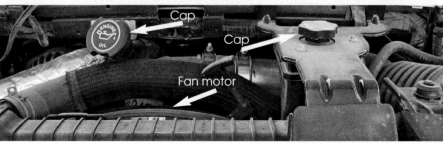

SUVs

Searching an SUV is much the same as searching a sedan or van, except that SUVs usually have more room between the wheels and the body of the vehicle, resulting in more places to hide things. Remember that an explosive device has to be attachable or able to sit on top of some part without falling off, but most new SUVs offer lots of places to put devices.

Underside

The underside inspection of the SUV must be even more thorough than one for a

You need to check the space between the wheels and the bottom of an SUV even more carefully than on a sedan or van. As usual, inspect the area around the tires for signs of tampering.

These two photos show just a few of the places in an SUV's wheel area where IEDs can be hidden.

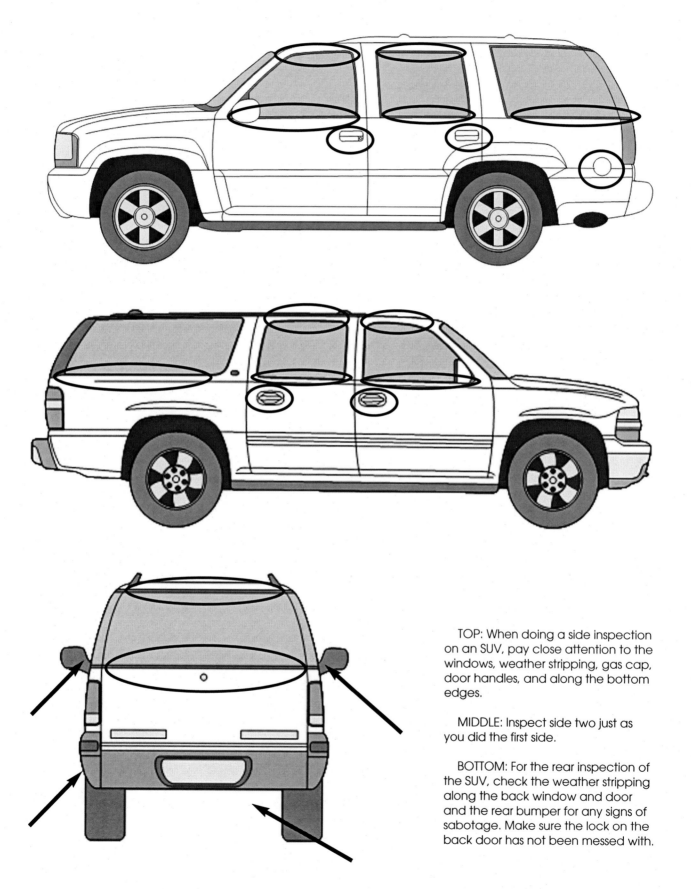

TOP: When doing a side inspection on an SUV, pay close attention to the windows, weather stripping, gas cap, door handles, and along the bottom edges.

MIDDLE: Inspect side two just as you did the first side.

BOTTOM: For the rear inspection of the SUV, check the weather stripping along the back window and door and the rear bumper for any signs of sabotage. Make sure the lock on the back door has not been messed with.

van, because the SUV has twice as many areas to hide or attach IEDs.

Interior

Perform the preentry interior inspection for an SUV the same way as for the van. The SUV also usually sits too high to get a good view of the interior. The procedures for checking the engine compartment on an SUV are the same as those for the sedan and the van.

• • •

In closing, it is up to you to know the vehicles in which you and your family will be riding, whether they are your own, belong to your company or agency, or are rentals. If a vehicle is a rental, take Polaroids so you can remember specific features and don't forget to mark wires and cables and notice the clean areas or dirty areas as required.

The exhaust pipe is a favorite place to stash an IED on all vehicles, including SUVs. Put a rod through the pipe or a grid over it to prevent someone from emplacing a device in your vehicle.

The underside of an SUV has twice as many places to hide an IED as a sedan or van, so your inspection must be very thorough.

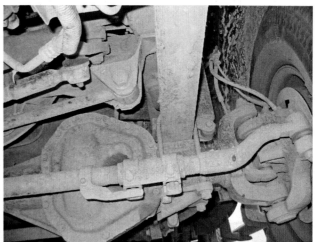

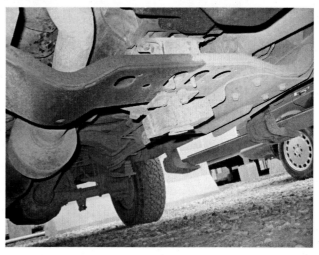

IED SEARCH

External Search

❑ Walk around the vehicle and look in the surrounding areas for disturbed terrain and standoff weapons and IEDs.

❑ Make sure the gas cap is still on; place a lock on the gas cap door.

❑ Look for signs of forced entry: broken windows, damaged locks, torn or ripped weather stripping.

❑ Check for foreign objects on ground or items discarded in haste or left behind, such as torn tape, bags, shaved or clipped wires, and batteries.

❑ If you are parked on a soft surface, look to see if the ground been disturbed. Are there any signs of tampering with the grounds: new soil, tread marks disturbed, scuff marks, or indentations?

❑ Are there any smudges on the body of the vehicle where people would need to lean against it or use part of the frame to pull themselves up?

❑ Look around and inside the hollow space of the bumper for objects.

❑ Check underneath the vehicle for any objects that have been added or tampered with.

❑ Check on top of the tires and along the axles for objects placed there.

❑ Do the tires have a nonhollow or inconsistent sound in the walls? Do they have a strange odor from the air valve? Is there a strange odor from the spare tire? Do they have unusually clean or dirty lug nuts or hubcaps compared to other wheels?

❑ Check the exhaust pipe for objects if you have not placed a screen or bolt through it.

❑ Ideally, your vehicle should not have wheel covers or hubcaps, but if you do, look for smudges, dirt, or scratches where someone may have removed and then replaced them.

❑ Check for items taped or attached to the frame.

❑ Are there any signs of recent installation of such components as a fuel tank, muffler, etc.?

Internal Search

❑ Look through the windows to search the interior; use all available window surfaces to view the widest possible area.

❑ When opening doors, remember to do this slowly, looking the whole time for trip wires or objects wedged between the seats and doors.

❑ Do the doors feel heavy when opened?

❑ Look under the dash for loose or added wiring, or objects that do not belong.

❑ Ideally, remove floor mats before departing the vehicle, but if they are present, check underneath for pressure devices, especially near the pedals.

❑ Check the roof lining for tampering, ripped or torn areas, and whether it's looser than it should be.

❑ Check headrest for tampering.

❑ Check sun visor for tampering.

❑ Ideally, you should not have a cover on your dome light; if you do have one, then you need to check for objects that may have been placed inside.

❑ Check under the front seat for items that may have been hidden there.

❑ Interior compartments (e.g., glove box, ashtray) should be left open, making them easier to check without having to open them during the search.

❑ If electrical components or LEDs are on when vehicle power is off, and they flicker on inspection, this could be an indication of tampering with your vehicle's electrical system.

❑ Are there any new, damaged, or scratched screws?

❑ Have the air vents been plugged?

❑ Is the blower broken or missing?

❑ Are there any unusual lumps or bulges in front and/or rear seats?

❑ Look at the front and/or rear seats to see if they are rigid.

Engine Compartment

❑ Open the engine compartment hood slowly, checking for trip wires or things attached to it.

❑ Check the battery for any added wires or cables.

❑ Check around the firewall for IEDs; this is where they have the greatest effect.

❑ Search any areas that are shut but can be opened to stash objects (e.g., air filter).

❑ Check for any odd or clean wires.

❑ Check cold air filter.

❑ Check freshly painted areas, new welds, shiny bolts, or sheet metal work on firewalls.

❑ Be suspicious of a clean engine in a dirty car.

❑ Does the hood feel heavy when opened and closed? (Reminder: have the driver pop open the hood, but you move the hood yourself.)

❑ Look for clean or wiped areas, wires, and screws.

Trunk Compartment

❑ Open the lid slowly, checking for trip wires or things attached to it.

❑ Ideally, you have removed all mats and false walls from the trunk, but if you have a mat, check underneath.

❑ Pay particular attention to the area behind the rear seat; this is the best place for an IED because the force blows into the passenger compartment.

❑ Check all wiring for turn signals, automatic trunk release, and brake and trunk lights. IEDs need a power source, and these are easy to access.

❑ Look under the spare tire and check the tire pressure to make sure it is correct. Always mark your spare tire so you know if it has been substituted or moved.

Electrical System

❑ Check carefully those systems that require electricity, since the wiring system in vehicles is easily available and power is one of the things required to explode an IED.

❑ Make sure your radio functions and all the preset channels are still loaded in. When someone tampers with your electrical system to add an explosive, tracking, or listening device, he has to disconnect the battery. Sometimes this will cause your radio to dump all its presets.

❑ Are the dashboard lights dim, flickering, or out? This could indicate tampering with the electrical system.

Miscellaneous

- ❑ Is there anything unusual in factory-built compartments?
- ❑ Check for new or shiny bolts and screws.
- ❑ Are there any unusual scratches, which could have been made by screwdrivers, wrenches, or similar tools?
- ❑ Broken parts or bent sheet metal could be signs of tampering.
- ❑ Unusually clean or dirty components and areas could indicate tampering.
- ❑ Is any wire or tape stored in the vehicle?
- ❑ New or broken welds could be signs of tampering.
- ❑ Look for unusual fingerprints of grease and/or oil in otherwise clean areas.
- ❑ Check for fresh bodywork (e.g., fresh fiberglassing, fresh paint).
- ❑ Fresh wiring and electrical tape are suspicious.
- ❑ Fresh undercoating, particularly on older vehicles, should be checked out.
- ❑ New caulking can be discovered by smell or touch.
- ❑ Check for missing or altered vehicle identification number.
- ❑ Are the headlights and taillights not working?
- ❑ Has the front grill been modified or had false compartments installed?
- ❑ Is there no access to front bumper cavity?
- ❑ Is the trunk lid heavy (i.e., loaded)?
- ❑ Can you smell caulk/glue or other strange odor?

TRUCKS

- ❑ Is the tailgate unusually heavy?
- ❑ Is there evidence of fresh paint or body filler/fiberglass?
- ❑ Does any part sound inconsistent or nonhollow when tapped?
- ❑ Does the floor seem unusually thick?

CHAPTER 16

Case Studies of Actual Vehicle Attacks

These case studies describe attacks against various targets throughout the world. The attackers gathered their intelligence and came up with a plan that exploited the weaknesses of their victims and their security. As you will see, very often the attacks were successful. A careful study of these cases will give you an insight into the thinking of terrorists and how they plan their attacks. You will also see how following the advice given in this book might have prevented some of these attacks or allowed the targets to escape uninjured.

EXPLOSIVE AMBUSHES

Adm. Luis Carrero Blanco, Spanish Prime Minister Madrid, Spain, 20 December 1973

The Euzkadi Ta Askatasuna (ETA—Basque Nation and Freedom) assassinated Adm. Luis Carrero Blanco, the Spanish prime minister, in Madrid, Spain, on 20 December 1973 using an explosive ambush. Initially the ETA had targeted Blanco for kidnapping. A group of terrorists traveled to Madrid from the Basque provinces in northern Spain. Through surveillance that lasted approximately one year, the terrorists ruled out kidnapping Admiral Blanco and instead opted to assassinate him.

The terrorists rented a basement apartment on Calle de Claudio Coello. Their cover story was that they were sculptors and would be making a lot of noise. They then began to chip through the concrete wall below street level and tunnel out underneath the street, a process that took eight days. They dug a T-shaped chamber for the 75 kilograms of explosives they would use. The top of the T was parallel to the road above, increasing their chances of killing the victim. After positioning the charge, they primed it electrically, ran the firing wire out the tunnel, and packed most of the removed dirt back into the tunnel to tamp the charge, giving the blast upward direction. Disguised as telephone repairmen, they ran the wire out the apartment and to the corner of Claudio Coello and Diego de Leon.

On the day of the attack, the terrorists parked a car with additional explosives inside, adjacent to the kill zone, as a marker. A lookout was stationed to give the signal to a second man positioned at the corner with a battery, ready to fire the charge. That morning Blanco followed his *daily routine*, which included a stop at a church before he proceeded to his office. He left the church, drove about one block, turned left onto Juan Bravo, and drove to the next corner, turning left onto

Calle de Claudio Coello. When the explosive charge went off, it blew Blanco's car over the five-story church he had just left. The car came to rest on a balcony inside the church courtyard. Blanco, his driver, and his security guard are said to have survived the blast and the landing, but Blanco and the guard died shortly afterward and the driver died en route to the hospital after rescue crews found them about two hours later. (The emergency workers thought that the vehicle had been destroyed; no one realized it had been blown onto the upper-story balcony.)

Immediately after the explosion, the terrorists ran from the scene yelling, "Gas! Gas!" causing further confusion and disguising their role in the attack. They then escaped from Madrid by vehicle. To exploit the act, the terrorists later wrote a book entitled *Operation Ogro: How and Why We Executed Carrero Blanco*, which was originally published in France and is still banned in Spain.

Gen. Alexander Haig, Supreme Allied Commander, Europe Brussels, Belgium, 25 June 1979

Members of the Red Army Faction (RAF) attempted to assassinate U.S. Gen. Alexander Haig on 25 June 1979 using an explosive ambush. The RAF, a terrorist organization based in West Germany (also known as the Baader-Meinhof Group), placed the general under surveillance about 30 days before the attempt. Through surveillance, the RAF determined that General Haig traveled in a three-car motorcade and varied the three possible routes to and from his office at Supreme Headquarters Allied Powers Europe (SHAPE) in Mons, Belgium. On the morning of the attack, construction had closed one of the three possible routes, which limited the choices of the security detail and enhanced the chances of the terrorists for success. The route taken that morning was the one most often used because it was the one preferred by the general.

The terrorists set up the ambush as follows. One terrorist on a motorcycle was positioned at a major intersection along the route. When it approached this intersection, the motorcade had two options: the vehicles could pass through the intersection and continue along the target route, or they could turn left onto an alternate route. From this location, the terrorists could determine which of the two routes the motorcade would take and radio to the personnel at the ambush site, who were located on a knoll overlooking a small bridge containing the explosive device. The triggering wire led from the device to a grassy knoll 150 meters away, where it was attached to a small, plastic battery pack and activated by a plastic toggle switch.

On the day of the attack, Haig left his residence at his usual time and took his preferred route to SHAPE. The motorcade consisted of the lead car, the general's armored Mercedes, and an unarmored follow car. After traveling about 3 miles along the route, the lead car was about 200 meters in front of the general's car, maintaining a speed of approximately 30 mph. As the general's car passed over the 50-foot bridge that held the explosive device, the terrorist on the knoll activated the device, setting off the explosives. At the time of the explosion, the follow car was about four car lengths behind the general's car. The blast caught only the very rear potion of Haig's car, causing little damage. The following car received most of the blast and was blown back 50 feet from the blast.

After the explosion, the general ordered his driver to stop because he was worried about the security personnel. Haig got out of the vehicle with the intention of assessing the situation, but his aide finally persuaded the general to get back into the car and leave the area, since the aide was sure that Haig was the primary target. Although the follow car sustained considerable damage, the passengers received only minor injuries.

The following are just a few of the many possible reasons the well-planned attack failed. The battery pack was located too far away from the device and was too slow to set off the charge. Bushes partially obstructed the attackers' view of the bridge. The general's driver was traveling at a higher rate of speed than normal. The terrorists only had a few seconds to visually acquire the target, judge the timing, and detonate their device.

An important side note to this incident was that the terrorists did not have the target area covered by small-arms fire. Had they done so, they could have assassinated the general when he exited the car. Terrorist groups learn from their mistakes very quickly and pass that knowledge on.

WEAPONS AMBUSHES

Gen. Frederick Kroesen, Commander in Chief, U.S. Army, Europe Heidelberg, Germany, 15 September 1981

One of the best-planned and -executed weapons attacks occurred on 15 September 1981, when the RAF attempted to kill Gen. Frederick Kroesen, Commander in Chief, U.S. Army, Europe.

Gudrun Ensslin, a commando of the RAF, and several other members planned and carried out the attack. The terrorists had prepared an ambush position about 138 yards from the attack site, which was at a traffic light at a major intersection in Heidelberg. The terrorists set up their firing position by following a path just below the Heidelberg University International Student Center. They then left this path and descended 54 yards by rope farther down the hill. About 100 yards from the end of the rope, they set up a dome-type tent and four sleeping bags. They lived there for about a week while they watched General Kroesen's movements. Eleven yards below their living area, they cleared a firing area in the brush just large enough to view the target area and avoid detection from below. They also set up a CB radio and antenna to communicate with other terrorists following the motorcade.

The general had a trained driver and an armored U.S. vehicle, but Heidelberg's mayor, upon learning of a threat to the general's life, had insisted that Kroesen accept his armored Mercedes and a former German police officer as a driver. This retired policeman had been a member of the city accident investigation team and had not been trained in protective driving; his only qualification for the job was that he spoke English. The general had been using the new driver and vehicle for about 30 days when the attack occurred.

The morning of the attack, the general was sitting in the rear seat with his wife, who normally did not ride with him but was on her way to a dentist's appointment. The German driver and the general's aide, Lieutenant Colonel Bodine, were in the front seat. A CID protective detail was in a follow car. An unidentified vehicle was in front of the general's car to make sure it stopped at the traffic light in the kill zone. This vehicle waited at a green light until it turned red and then drove through it. At the time no one thought this was suspicious.

As the general's partially armored Mercedes and his unarmored follow car stopped at the light, the general's driver shut off his engine (required in Germany to save gas and cut down on emissions). The vehicle in front of the general's car then drove off, and a young blonde woman standing on the corner across from the general's vehicle pulled out a pistol and fired several rounds into the driver's-side glass in an attempt to kill the driver. At this time two rounds from an RPG-7 and four 7.62mm rounds came from the terrorists' position on the hill. The first RPG round hit the road 2 meters behind the vehicle; the second round missed the passenger compartment and detonated when it hit the trunk. Both rounds had been fired within approximately 20 seconds, indicating that the ambushers were trained. After the two RPG rounds were fired, a terrorist on a motor scooter drove by and fired an automatic weapon at the follow car and the general's car. The 7.62mm rounds struck the front window on the driver's side, the left rear window, and the top of the roof just above the general's head but did not cause any damage. General Kroesen received minor lacerations on the back of his neck, and his wife suffered a slight hearing loss. The untrained German driver, who had turned off the ignition to save gas, froze and did not attempt any evasive maneuvers until the general's aide physically shook him to get him to start the car and leave the site. If the general's vehicle had not been armored or fitted with bullet-resistant glass, General Kroesen, his wife, and the front-seat occupants would have been killed.

One of the important things about this attack is the use of small-arms fire directed at the rear of the vehicle after the RPG rounds were fired, as if the terrorists expected the general to exit the vehicle and assess the situation. This demonstrated that the terrorists had taken the lessons learned from the failed assassination attempt of General Haig and applied them to another type of attack against another U.S. general.

Lt. Cdr. Albert Schaufelberger, U.S. Military Group San Salvador, El Salvador, 25 May 1983

Lt. Cdr. Albert Schaufelberger, the senior U.S. Naval representative at the U.S. Military Group, El Salvador, had been dating an employee of the university, Ms. Consuelo Escalante Aguilera, for several months and had become time and place predictable. He had established a pattern of driving to the university in civilian clothes to pick her up after work. Although he did this on different days of the week, the time he picked her up was always the same, between 1830 and 1840 hours. On 25 May he arrived at his usual time and honked the horn. This was Schaufelberger's signal to inform Aguilera that he had arrived, whereupon she would walk out to his car. As Aguilera left her office, she observed a white Volkswagen microbus pull up and stop near Schaufelberger's car, an armored Ford Maverick provided by the U.S. Embassy. Three men got out of the bus while a fourth man stayed with the vehicle, which was still running. One of the men approached Aguilera, which focused Schaufelberger's attention on what was going

on between the man and his girlfriend. The other gunman, carrying a revolver, went behind Schaufelberger's car, walked up to the driver's-side door, and fired four rounds of .22 magnum from a handgun into the left side of Schaufelberger's head. The attackers then jumped into their vehicle and escaped.

So how did this unfortunate incident occur with a well-trained Navy SEAL in an armored car? For one thing, the air conditioner in Schaufelberger's vehicle was broken, and instead of having it fixed he had removed the bullet-resistant Lexgard glass on the driver's side. He always traveled with a revolver underneath his right leg while driving, so it would be ready if he needed it; however, the one time he did need it, he never got the chance to use it. He allowed himself to become distracted and focused his attention on his girlfriend instead of observing what was taking place around him. Plus, he was time and place predictable to the threat surveillance and assault element.

Union Texas Petroleum Executives, Karachi, Pakistan, 12 November 1997

On the morning of 12 November 1997, four U.S. employees of the Houston-based Union Texas Petroleum Corporation and their driver left their hotel in Karachi, Pakistan. As they drove across a bridge in the center of the city's commercial sector, a red Honda intercepted their black Toyota station wagon, which their company had provided. Two men dressed in traditional Pakistani *salwar kameez* (baggy trousers and long shirts) got out of the Honda, quickly approached the station wagon, and opened fire with the automatic weapons they carried. The occupants of the station wagon never had a chance to react; they died less than 600 yards from their hotel.

A witness to the attack said he heard something that sounded like a car accident. "I turned and saw to my horror that two men had come out of the car with guns. They started shooting." The witness at this point sought shelter behind a Dumpster. "When I peeped out from behind the

Dumpster, one of them was checking the people inside. He then changed the gun's magazine and fired a couple of more shots . . . I have been seeing shootings and killings in this city for years now, but the guys who attacked the Americans looked professional. They finished the whole thing in a matter of minutes. They checked the people inside the car and throughout the process were very relaxed, even when they got back into their car and left."

This was the second time in 2 1/2 years that an attack on Americans had taken place in Karachi. In March 1995 two U.S. consulate staffers were shot dead using the same tactics. Before this attack on the oil executives in November 1997, the U.S. Embassy had issued warnings to Americans living and working in Pakistan because of the conviction of Mir Aimal Kasi, a Pakistani who killed two CIA employees in front of the CIA headquarters in McLean, Virginia, in 1993.

Pakistani law enforcement officials linked the subsequent killings to Kasi's conviction and believe it could even be connected to the conviction of Ramzi Ahmed Yousef, who was extradited from Pakistan in 1995 in connection with the 1993 World Trade Center bombing.

These American businessmen had no defensive training, lived in a hotel frequented by Americans, and drove in the same vehicle every day with an untrained driver using the same routes to and from their work location.

Hans-Martin Schleyer, Cologne, Germany, 5 September 1977

Hans-Martin Schleyer was the leading German industrialist, the chairman of the board at Mercedes-Benz, the head of the German Association of Industry, and a close personal friend and advisor to the chancellor of Germany, Helmut Schmidt. As early as 1975, German police had known that Schleyer was a likely target for terrorist attack because the police investigation into the shooting of German banker Robert Jurgen Ponto in 1977 revealed that Schleyer had been an alternate

target. After discovering that information, the police gave Schleyer maximum protection, including personal bodyguards and a 24-hour guard on his residence. When traveling, he moved in a security motorcade and rode in an armored car.

On 5 September 1977 Schleyer and his driver were headed home in a motorcade from his office in Cologne. Schleyer and his driver were in the lead vehicle, a Mercedes, with Schleyer riding in the right rear seat. Three bodyguards followed in another Mercedes. As his motorcade, traveling along a well-established route, turned right onto a one-way street, a car heading in the wrong direction forced the lead car to swerve to one side, where a terrorist was waiting with a baby carriage. The attacker then pushed the baby carriage in front of the lead car, which caused the driver to swerve and collide with the original blocking car. On one side of the street was parked a Volkswagen (VW) microbus with more terrorists inside.

Once the motorcade was effectively stopped, six terrorists got out of the blocking car and the VW bus, firing on both vehicles in the motorcade and killing all three of the bodyguards in the follow car and Schleyer's driver in less than 90 seconds. They then removed Schleyer and made their escape with the target in the VW. The terrorists used a variety of weapons, including shotguns, machine pistols, and a MAC-10 submachine gun.

The RAF kidnappers demanded the release of jailed RAF terrorists in exchange for Schleyer's safety. Two of the RAF's main members in captivity were Andreas Baader and Ulrike Meinhof. The German authorities would not meet RAF demands.

In an attempt to demonstrate international solidarity among terrorist groups, four members of the Popular Front for the Liberation of Palestine (PFLP) hijacked a Lufthansa 737 jet to increase pressure on the German government to give in to the RAF demands and release its members held in custody. In response, the German police stormed the plane as it sat in Mogadishu, Somalia, killing the terrorists and freeing the hostages.

When the RAF members in prison heard of the failed hijacking, they became depressed and committed suicide. When this happened, the terrorists holding Schleyer killed him on 18 October 1977, after 43 days of captivity.

How did the terrorists carry out such a successful operation against someone who knew he was a target and was also protected by the police? To begin with, Schleyer and his bodyguards made serious mistakes that the terrorists used to their advantage. The most critical mistake was never varying the route of the motorcade to and from work and having only slight variations in time. Also, the follow car was much too close to the lead vehicle, which allowed no room for maneuvering around the lead vehicle to engage the threat. Finally, Schleyer's driver stopped his car instead of ramming the vehicle that was blocking the road; if he had run up on the curb and rammed the lead vehicle or run over the lady with the baby carriage, the victims might have escaped with their lives.

Leamon R. Hunt,
Director General of the Multinational
Force and Observers in the Sinai Peninsula
Rome, Italy, 1984

Leamon R. Hunt, the Director General of the Multinational Force and Observers (MFO) in the Sinai Peninsula, was assassinated in front of his residence in Rome by the Fighting Communist Party, a group usually identified with the Red Brigades urban terrorists. Hunt was a career U.S. diplomat, having served 32 years in the Foreign Service before becoming the director general of the peacekeeping force.

Hunt did not have a security team, but he had a chauffeur and traveled in a hardened (armored) vehicle. He had left his NATO office in Rome and was approaching the small villa where he lived when he was attacked. Hunt's villa had a very tall wall around the entire residence and an iron gate located at the entrance. This electronic gate took approximately 30 seconds to open once it was activated. On the evening of the ambush, the driver stopped at the gate to wait for it to open. A car pulled up behind the armored vehicle, and terrorists got out and began firing an automatic weapon at the vehicle.

The chauffeur, who was not trained in security and had no evasive/defensive driving training, told Hunt to get down in his seat, and the chauffeur himself hunkered down in his seat while the terrorist continued firing on the vehicle. If the chauffeur had been trained in defensive driving, he could have used the vehicle as a weapon and backed up into the terrorist and then driven away, or he could have just turned the wheel sharply and driven away. Both the chauffeur and Hunt are believed to have gone into shock, since Hunt never did hide in his seat. They sat there for several minutes while the attackers fired approximately two magazines from the submachine gun on their vehicle.

The terrorists then got into another car and used their preplanned escape route. Hunt was hit when shrapnel from a round finally penetrated the bullet-resistant glass. The chauffeur went to the house to get help and then finally took Hunt to the hospital, where he died about an hour after arrival.

The chauffeur is mostly to blame for the success of this attack, because he failed to use his vehicle as a weapon or to get Hunt out of the kill zone. This is a common occurrence in such attacks because the drivers are untrained and either do nothing or do the wrong thing, making the situation worse. Every chauffeur and security driver needs to be trained in evasive driving and attack recognition. The more training they have, the less apt they are to freeze up during an attack, especially during the vital initial seconds.

Armored vehicles are bullet resistant, not bulletproof, and most manufacturers only guarantee them for three rounds of a certain diameter. Depending on the level of the armor, it can be three rounds in 1 inch or 1/2 inch, but eventually bullets will penetrate. That's why it is so important to *move*.

EN ROUTE KIDNAPPINGS

Aldo Moro,
Former Italian Prime Minister
Rome, Italy, 16 March 1978

Aldo Moro, the former Italian prime minister and then leader of the Christian Democratic Party, was trying to form a coalition government with the Italian Communist Party, and he was due at the Italian parliament on the morning of 16 March 1978 to vote on that issue. The Red Brigades, who opposed this idea, had originally decided to kidnap the head of the Italian Communist Party, Enrico Berlinguer, but his security profile was too high. They focused instead on the secondary target, Aldo Moro, whose security profile was not as high. In other words, Moro was a softer, more predictable target.

On the Tuesday of the attack, at about 0820 hours, Moro was picked up in front of his home in Rome by his usual car and a police escort. His personal security detail included an armed driver and a bodyguard riding in the lead vehicle (Moro rode in the right rear seat). The police escort acted as the follow car and had an armed driver and two armed police bodyguards. The security personnel had all been assigned submachine guns, but these were stored in the trunk— Moro didn't like these guns and insisted on their being in the trunk—so only their handguns were readily accessible.

Moro was a man of simple, methodical habits, and for 15 years he more or less traveled the same route from his home to his office, making him time and place predictable. Every morning he stopped for a few minutes at the church of San Francesco d'Assisi or at the chapel Santa Chiara. On this morning he stopped at San Francisco d'Assisi at 0830 hours. At 0900, Moro and his motorcade left the church and continued on their way to the parliament.

Somewhere along the route, a white Fiat 128 station wagon with diplomatic license plates moved in front of Moro's motorcade. Two other cars, a blue and a white Fiat sedan, moved in some distance behind the motorcade. At about 0905 hours, as the motorcade approached a stop sign, the station wagon in front of the motorcade stopped suddenly. Moro's car was traveling too fast and too close to the station wagon to stop, and it hit the station wagon in the rear. Moro's follow car, also traveling too fast and too close, rammed into the rear of Moro's car, pinning it between the two vehicles, with no chance of escape.

During the surveillance phase, the terrorists had determined that both Moro's driver and the driver of the follow car routinely tailgated, and they used this to their advantage. The RB had also parked a car along the curb next to the planned attack site to ensure that Moro's car would be blocked from possible escape.

After the crash, two men got out of the vehicle that Moro's car had rear-ended as if to inspect the damage. They were carrying gym bags, from which they pulled pistols and started firing through the front-side windows of Moro's car, killing Moro's driver and the bodyguard.

At the instant of collision, a second attack element—four men dressed in Alitalia (Italian Airlines) uniforms who had been standing in front of a closed bar as if waiting for a bus to the airport (since many airline personnel lived in the area this did not seem suspicious)—pulled weapons from their flight bags and rushed toward Moro's follow car. They killed the driver and the bodyguard, who were riding in the front seat, before the two could draw their weapons. The third bodyguard, who had been riding in the right rear seat of the follow car, managed to get out of the rear door and fire three rounds before he was killed. His three shots wounded two of the terrorists, before he himself was killed by what is believed to have been a security element stationed near the side of the road in the trees.

This was the only miscalculation the terrorists made: their intelligence had indicated that the second bodyguard usually sat in the left rear seat of the follow car, which is where they concentrated their fire. But on this day a new man was on the detail, and he sat on the opposite side.

A third element, consisting of two terrorists, was hiding behind a row of bushes in front of the bar. A few seconds after the start of the attack, these two men jumped out, ran toward Moro's car, pulled him from the backseat, and led him to a waiting blue Fiat. This was the same car that had been trailing the Moro motorcade at a distance. Just after the collision, this car and the white Fiat moved into the attack area to help with the getaway. The terrorists also had another car parked around the corner from the bar. When the attack was over, this car acted as the lead vehicle, followed by the blue Fiat carrying Moro and the white Fiat containing the other terrorists.

From start to finish, the whole attack lasted no more than 30 seconds and involved at least 12 terrorists, who fired between 80 and 90 rounds, killing five bodyguards. The military-style operation employed excellent surveillance, reconnaissance, deception, and detailed planning. The use of such sound operational concepts as surprise, violence, and superior firepower, as well as planned escape routes, made this one of the most successful and studied terrorist incidents of our time.

The RB did several things to limit the number of innocent bystanders and to confuse the police before, during, and after the operation. They slashed the tires of the flower vendor who normally was in the planned attack zone. They overloaded telephone lines during the attack and used false alerts to further scatter the police during the postincident phase, keeping the police from concentrating on the real incident.

In exchange for Moro's release, the RB demanded the release of 13 terrorists. Prime Minister Andreotti refused to deal with the terrorists. On 9 May, 55 days after he was abducted, Aldo Moro was found shot to death in a Renault station wagon in central Rome. The car was found in the exact middle of the Via Caetani, the street on which the headquarters of both the Italian Communist Party and the Christian Democratic Party are located.

Giovanni Enrico Bucher, Swiss Ambassador to Brazil Rio de Janeiro, Brazil, 7 December 1970

During his stay in Rio de Janeiro, Giovanni Enrico Bucher, the Swiss ambassador to Brazil, had established a definite pattern of traveling between his office and his residence. He always traveled the same route at the same time of day, and his limited security consisted of only one guard—despite being warned repeatedly that he had been targeted for a terrorist attack. The attack finally came on 7 December 1970.

The attack site was on a narrow, heavily traveled, one-way street. The terrorists used a total of four vehicles in the execution of their ambush, with approximately seven to ten armed men involved. The entire sequence of events lasted less than a minute from beginning to end.

As the ambassador's vehicle turned onto the road and proceeded in the direction of the attack site, vehicle one (a Volkswagen) established a roadblock behind the target's to provide security and prevent any interference with the actions about to take place. Vehicle two (another Volkswagen) and vehicle three (a lightweight pickup truck) were parked on the opposite side of the street facing in the wrong direction. Vehicle four (also a Volkswagen) was parked along the side of the attack site about 50 feet from the entrance into the preplanned attack zone.

Vehicle two, on the opposite side of the street, made a sharp U-turn in front of the ambassador's approaching car, causing the ambassador's driver to brake sharply and come to a complete stop. Vehicle three then moved into position at the rear of the ambassador's vehicle, blocking it from behind. The attackers encircled the target car, killed the ambassador's guard, quickly transferred the ambassador to vehicle four, and fled the attack site using their pre-planned escape route.

Even with all the personnel and coordination involved, the attack from start to finish lasted only 1 minute. This indicates that the threat had excellent intelligence on the victim's movements and had rehearsed the attack many times before the kidnapping actually took place. Before the car was stopped and blocked in, the ambassador's driver attempted no evasive maneuvers or defensive driving techniques. In fact, he did not move the vehicle at all after it was stopped.

OVERRUN ATTACKS

Col. James Rowe,
U.S. Military Advisory Group
Manila, Philippines, 21 April 1989

During the early morning hours of 21 April 1989, members of the New People's Army (NPA) of the Philippines assassinated Col. James Rowe, chief of the ground forces division of the Joint U.S. Military Advisory Group (JUSMAG) in Manila.

Colonel Rowe and his family were aware of the terrorist threat against him before the attack. While living openly in a Manila suburb, Rowe did attempt to decrease the chances of attack by varying the routes he used to and from work. However, the NPA had determined that Rowe's routes, although varied, usually led to one key choke point that he had to pass through.

On the morning of the attack, as the 51-year-old colonel's vehicle entered the choke point, a traffic circle less than a mile from the Military Advisory Group headquarters, two hooded gunmen on a motor bike pulled alongside his vehicle and fired. Rowe's vehicle was lightly armored, and of the twenty-one 5.56mm bullets fired, only one managed to penetrate the rear compartment. Unfortunately, this bullet struck the colonel in the back of the head, it is believed as he was ducking. He died on the way to the hospital.

Rowe's Filipino driver, who was injured in the attack as well, had not received any prior defensive driving training, and he is believed to have panicked and frozen up during the attack. After the attack, the driver attended the evasive driving school at Fort Bragg, North Carolina. During this training, he froze up during every scenario presented to him. It should also be noted that the vehicle Rowe was riding in was modified locally with armor, and the round that struck him penetrated an unarmored portion of the vehicle. Ironically, Colonel Rowe had started the antiterrorism program and driving school that his Filipino driver later attended and was himself well versed in defensive driving tactics.

Know your driver's training and abilities!

M.Sgt. Robert Judd,
Athens, Greece, 3 April 1984

While stopped at a light on his way to the Hellenikon Air Force Base near the Athens airport on 3 April 1984, M.Sgt. Robert Judd noticed a motorcycle weaving slowly through the cars behind him. Judd paid attention because both the driver and passenger were wearing helmets and masks, which was almost never seen in Greece at that time, and also most scooters and motorcycles drove to the front of the line at traffic lights, and this one was hanging back and going very slowly.

As he watched, Judd saw the passenger on the motorcycle pull something shiny from a bag. It was a pistol, and as the two masked gunmen on a motorcycle got closer the passenger started shooting at him. Judd was hit twice before he hit the gas and drove over the median into oncoming traffic, thereby evading and disrupting the attacker's plan. As he drove away, the gunman fired at least three more shots through the rear window of his station wagon. Judd was wounded in the hand and lung by two .45-caliber bullets.

The Greek terrorist organization Revolutionary Organization 17 November (commonly referred to as 17 November) claimed responsibility for the attack, saying that it attacked Judd to protest the Greek government's failure to remove four U.S. military bases in Greece.

Judd's observation of what was taking place around him, his recognition that the actions of the motorcycle riders appeared out of place, his strict attention to a possible threat, and his instinctive movement out of the kill zone when the attack took place saved his life.

Capt. George Tsantes, Joint U.S. Military Aid Group Athens, Greece, 15 November 1983

After his arrival for assignment in Greece, Capt. George Tsantes was appointed as a chief of the naval section of the Joint U.S. Military Aid Group to Greece (JUSMAGG), which administers U.S. military aid programs. JUSMAGG had acquired a reputation among Greeks for working with the CIA to influence domestic politics, but this was mostly rumored rather than factual. A week before the attack on Tsantes, several left-wing newspapers stated that Captain Tsantes was a CIA agent, and they further speculated that he might be the CIA station chief in Athens. The U.S. Embassy denied these allegations, but the damage had already been done: Captain Tsantes had become a high-profile target.

Even after the articles appeared, however, neither the embassy nor Tsantes intensified his security procedures. Additionally, the captain had become predictable in his daily patterns: every weekday at 0700 hours, Tsantes used an embassy-provided black Plymouth sedan and chauffeur to travel the same route from his home in Kifissia, Greece, to his office, about 30 minutes away.

On 15 November 1983, his daily commute to work was dramatically different. Two men on a light blue Vespa motor scooter shadowed Tsantes as he drove. When his vehicle stopped at a traffic light, the scooter sped up alongside, and a gunman riding on the rear of the cycle fired seven shots from a .45-caliber pistol. Captain Tsantes was killed instantly, and his driver, 62-year-old Nikolaos Veloutsos, died at the hospital. The coroner's report stated that Tsantes died from a bullet directly below the heart, as well as one in the shoulder and a third one in the abdomen.

In taking credit for the assassination, the November 17 terrorist group claimed that it targeted Captain Tsantes because "he was one of the highest-ranking tools of American Imperialism in Greece." The group also said that the JUSMAGG, through its tools inside and outside the state bureaucracy, was responsible for numerous crimes against the Greek people.

This attack was successful because neither Tsantes nor the U.S. Embassy took any measures to increase his security after the accusations linking him to the CIA: his car was not armored, his driver was untrained, and Tsantes had no security detail.

ASSAULTS ON ARMORED VEHICLES

Assuming that armored vehicles cannot be defeated is a deadly misconception held by many people. Just take a look at what's going on in Iraq and you will see the insurgents coming up with new ways to defeat the unarmored and armored vehicles that coalition forces use daily. One of the reasons that the threat performs surveillance is to see what security you have and come up with ways to defeat it.

An excellent historical case study of this is the assassination of Alfred Herrhausen by the Red Army Faction in Germany.

Alfred Herrhausen, Chairman of the Deutsche Bank Frankfurt, Germany, 30 November 1989

Alfred Herrhausen was the chairman of the Deutsche Bank, the largest bank in Germany. But Herrhausen was much more than a banker; he was also considered Germany's senior industrialist and the most influential economic strategist in Germany. Plus he was a personal friend and an economic advisor to the chancellor of West Germany.

Herrhausen, 59 years old, lived in a very quiet, exclusive residential suburb of Frankfurt. On 30 November 1989 he left his residence at his normal time, approximately 0830, in his usual three-vehicle security convoy and headed toward his workplace, along the same route that he always took. As his lead security vehicle passed the attack site nothing happened, but as Herrhausen's armored car entered, a bike located on the side of the road exploded with around 22 pounds of TNT. The explosion propelled shrapnel through the right rear door, forcing a piece of the armored door into Herrhausen and pushing him across the backseat into the left door. The explosion took place less than 4 feet from the right rear door, where Herrhausen always sat. The force of the explosion threw his 2 1/2-ton vehicle across the street almost 83 feet and could be heard more 500 yards away. Herrhausen bled to death from his injuries, his driver was slightly hurt, and no other casualties were reported.

The planning to defeat this specific type of armored vehicle was extensive. The terrorists used a child's bike to set the shape-charged explosive so it would be at the right level to go off next to the door, and placed the explosive on the side of the street where Herrhausen usually rode in the back of the vehicle. This whole plan was designed to take out one person in his armored car, and it worked.

USMC Armored Van, Santiago, Chile, 16 February 1991

In Santiago, Chile, on 16 February 1991 the Manuel Rodriguez Patriotic Front (FPMR) terrorist group set up an attack on a U.S. Marine Corps security detachment armored van as it was leaving the Marine house residence. Once again, the threat's surveillance had provided the terrorists with the tactics to use.

A vehicle carrying a driver and three other men drove up and blocked the residence gate as the van carrying Marines was leaving the house. When the vehicle stopped, two men got out and attacked the armored van with small-arms fire, wounding one Marine when the bullet-resistant glass shattered. A fourth terrorist exited the car and fired a light antitank weapon, which hit the van but failed to detonate since it was fired too close to the target and didn't arm. The attackers then got in the vehicle and drove away.

Israeli Brig. Gen. Erez Gerstein, Southern Lebanon, 28 February 1999

On 28 February 1999, Israeli Brig. Gen. Erez Gerstein, his driver, a radio operator, and a news reporter were killed when a roadside bomb detonated against their armored Mercedes sedan in southern Lebanon. General Gerstein's vehicle was the lead car in an Israeli Defense Forces (IDF) convoy that was traveling in the eastern sector of the established security zone in south Lebanon. Gerstein, 38, was the highest-ranking Israeli officer to die in Lebanon since the 1982 Israeli invasion. His vehicle, which was an armor-plated Mercedes, careened off the road after the attack, rolled into the valley below, and burst into flames.

Chilean President Augusto Pinochet, Chile, 7 September 1986

On 7 September 1986 President Augusto Pinochet and his 10-year-old grandson narrowly escaped death while en route from Pinochet's country home to Santiago. Pinochet's motorcade was ambushed by 12 terrorists from the Manuel Rodriguez Patriotic Front. Armed with automatic rifles, rocket launchers, bazookas, and grenades, the attackers killed five and wounded eleven members of Pinochet's police and military escort in the attack. Pinochet sustained only minor injuries because he was riding in an armored Mercedes, and the driver was able to get the vehicle out of the kill zone and to Pinochet's house.

The threat had conducted surveillance to develop this well-conceived plan. The attack took place at a choke point at a bridge, and the attackers used a vehicle to block the lead convoy vehicle and another to block the rear vehicle. A well-aimed rocket destroyed the first vehicle in the convoy, as the attackers fired down on it from two sides. The quick-thinking, *trained* driver of Pinochet's vehicle backed it out of the kill zone, ramming the threat vehicle that was blocking the exit, and got his passengers safely back to Pinochet's residence. The vehicle was hit by more than 50 rounds of small-arms fire, which shattered several of the bulletproof windows, and light antitank weapons fire also struck the vehicle but did not explode because it was fired too close by the attacker and did not have the proper distance to arm.

Robert Kruger,
U.S. Ambassador to Burundi
Cibitoke Province, 14 June 1995

On 14 June 1995, a convoy carrying Robert Kruger, the U.S. Ambassador to the Central African Republic of Burundi, was attacked as it traveled on a mountain road in the province of Cibitoke.

The ambush site was well planned. The ambassador's convoy was made up of eight vehicles total. The lead vehicle was disabled by a grenade as it rounded a corner, and then the attackers started targeting all vehicles with automatic weapons fire, disabling the third vehicle in the convoy. This halted the convoy in the kill zone and exposed all the vehicles to the attackers' fire. The ambassador's vehicle had come to a stop too close to the vehicle in front of it, and the driver panicked and did not respond to the demands of the regional security officer (RSO) to back up.

The RSO took control of the vehicle from the passenger's side, backed it up, and then drove the vehicle around the stopped convoy and out of the kill zone. The second embassy vehicle followed the first and got out of the kill zone, heading toward the closest safe haven, which was the town of Butara. There the security personnel dropped off the wounded for treatment at a military facility and proceeded to the next safe haven in the town of Kayanza, where they stayed overnight in a secure location. The next morning they traveled back to the embassy by military helicopter.

The number of attackers is unknown, but two members of the convoy were killed and 13 were injured. From the time the attack started to the time the RSO took control of the ambassador's vehicle to escape the area the entire incident lasted less than 30 seconds.

• • •

As you can see from the above examples, armored cars no longer present much of an operational obstacle to attackers. Once they know that an armored vehicle is part of your security plan, they will find a way to defeat it. The most important thing you can do for your security during movement is to have a trained driver or become trained yourself, so that you know what to do in specific situations.

As I have emphasized throughout this book, most of the time this is simply to *move*. You should never allow your vehicle to get stopped. Once you are stopped and have no other security support, the attackers can take their time to get your vehicle open and take you out. And if they have done their surveillance and planning correctly, they will know exactly how to defeat your armored vehicle. Besides, if you are in an environment where you need an armored car for daily transport with a bodyguard, then you probably need to have security vehicles moving with you also.

About the Author

Bob Deatherage joined the U.S. Marines at 18, served three years, and then tried civilian life before enlisting in the U.S. Army. He spent 17 years in U.S. Army special operations, 14 as a Green Beret. He retired as the noncommissioned officer in charge of the antiterrorism training detachment located at the Special Warfare Center and School in Fort Bragg, North Carolina.

After retiring from the military, he worked as a security manager for a private contractor throughout Iraq. He is now conducting driver training, combat marksmanship, and antiterrorism training for the military, government, and law enforcement agencies throughout the United States.